# JOSHUA JAY'S
## AMAZING BOOK OF
# CARDS

### BY
### JOSHUA JAY

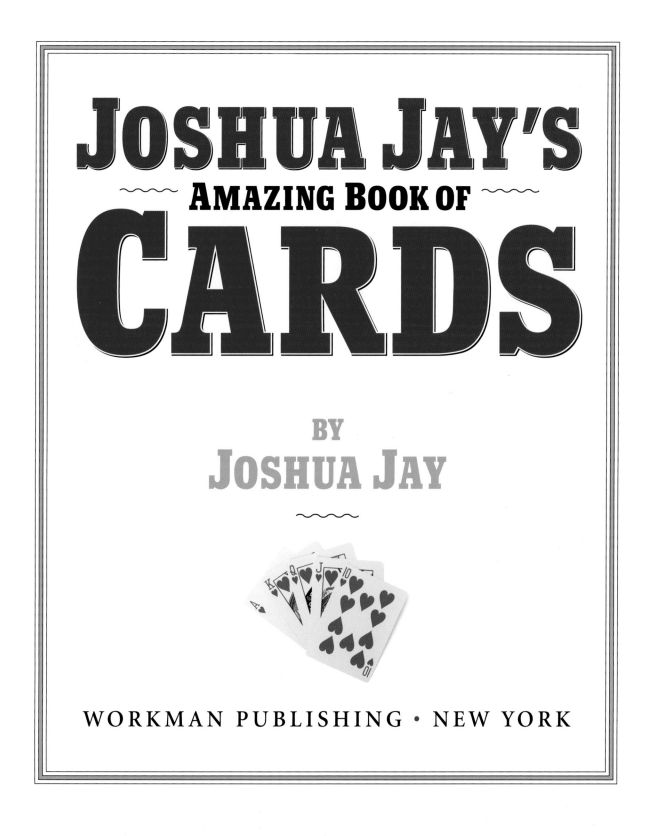

WORKMAN PUBLISHING · NEW YORK

Library of Congress Cataloging-in-Publication Data is available.

ISBN 978-0-7611-5842-4

Workman books are available at special discounts when purchased in bulk for premiums and sales promotions as well as for fund-raising or educational use. Special editions of book excerpts can also be created to specification. For details, contact the Special Sales Director at the address below or send an email to specialmarkets@workman.com.

Cover design by Robert Perino
Interior design by Julie Duquet

Workman Publishing Company, Inc.
225 Varick Street
New York, NY 10014-4381
workman.com
WORKMAN is a registered trademark of Workman Publishing Co., Inc.

Printed in China
First printing May 2010

10 9 8 7 6 5 4 3

## Photography Credits

Cover photograph composite: Evan Sklar.

Original photography by David Arky: pgs. v, 8, 9, 10, 11, 12 (top), 13, 14 (all on left), 15, 16 (top left & top right), 17, 18, 19, 20, 21 (all on left), 22, 23 (top & middle), 24, 25 (top left & top right), 26, 27 (top left & bottom left), 28, 29 (top left & top right), 30, 31, 33, 34 (bottom left & bottom right), 35 (bottom left & bottom right), 36, 37, 40, 41, 42, 43 (top), 44, 45, 46, 47 (all on left), 48, 49, 50, 51, 52, 53, 55 (bottom), 56, 57, 58, 59, 60, 62, 63, 64, 66, 67 (top left, top right, bottom left), 68, 69, 72, 73, 74 (top left & top right), 75, 76, 77, 78, 79, 80 (top left & bottom left), 81, 82, 83, 84, 85, 88, 89 (top left & top right), 90, 91, 93, 94, 95, 96, 97, 100, 101, 102, 103 (top), 104, 105, 107, 108, 109, 110 (left), 111, 113, 114 (top left & top right), 115, 117, 118, 119, 121, 122, 126, 127, 128 (top left & bottom left), 129, 130, 134, 135, 136, 137, 138, 139, 140, 141, 142, 143, 146, 147, 148, 149, 150, 155, 156, 157 (left), 158, 159, 162, 163, 166, 167, 168, 169, 170, 171 (top), 172, 173, 174, 175, 176, 177, 178, 179, 180, 181, 182, 183, 184, 185 (top left & top right).

Original photography by Joshua Jay and Eric Ryan Anderson: pgs. ii, viii, 3, 4, 6, 23 (bottom), 32, 34 (top), 38, 43 (bottom), 47 (right), 61, 67 (bottom right), 70, 80 (right), 86, 87, 89 (bottom), 98, 106, 112, 114 (bottom), 116, 120, 123, 124, 131, 132, 133, 144, 154, 160, 164, 165, 171 (bottom left & bottom right), 186, 200.

Original photography by Evan Sklar: pgs. 35 (top left & top right), 74 (bottom).

Cardstacker.com p. 157 (right); Courtesy of Cláudio Décourt p. 14 (bottom), p. 25 (bottom row), p. 92 (top), p. 103 (bottom row); Dover Publications, Inc. p. 1, p. 7, p. 71, p. 92 (bottom row), p. 99, p. 125, p. 145, p. 161, p. 187; Courtesy of Jason England p. 185 (bottom); From the collection of Steve Forte p. 16 (bottom row); Chris Mattison/Getty Images p. 12 (bottom); Mary Evans Picture Library/The Image Works p. 128 (right); Courtesy of The International Brotherhood of Magicians p. 189 (top left); Courtesy of Joshua Jay p. 65; Courtesy of Ralf Laue p. 21 (right), Melissa Lucier p. iii, p. 188; Mary Evans Picture Library p. 27 (right); Courtesy of Bruce T. Samboy p. 29 (bottom); Courtesy of The Society for American Magicians p. 189 (bottom left); Sophia Su: p. 54, p. 110 (right), p. 151.

# CONTENTS

*Foreword by David Blaine*.................................... **vii**

## INTRODUCTION
Playing Card Basics ................................. **1**

## CHAPTER 1

## ALL HANDS ON DECK
The Ribbon Spread and Flip* ....................... **8**

One-Handed Flip* ..................................... **10**

No-Handed Flip* ....................................... **11**

No-Handed Flip Plus* ............................... **13**

Two-Handed Fan* ..................................... **15**

Blank Fan* ................................................ **17**

Giant Fan* ............................................... **19**

One-Handed Fan* ..................................... **22**

One-Handed Cut* ..................................... **24**

Self-Cutting Deck* ................................... **26**

Catch-a-Deck ........................................... **28**

Throwing Cards* ....................................... **30**

Card Cascade ........................................... **33**

The Ultimate Catch .................................. **36**

## CHAPTER 2

## TRICKS
The Card Shark* ....................................... **40**

One Ahead* .............................................. **44**

The Ten-Twenty Force ............................... **48**

Finding Four Aces Without
   Touching the Deck ................................. **50**

Pointer Power* ......................................... **55**

Barely Lift a Finger* ................................. **58**

Presto Prediction* .................................... **62**

Friction Four* ........................................... **66**

Christmas Card ........................................ **68**

**\*** = *on companion DVD*

## CHAPTER 3
# SHUFFLE BORED

Hindu Shuffle* .................................... 72
Tabled Riffle Shuffle* .......................... 75
In-the-Hands Riffle Shuffle* ................ 78
Overhand Shuffle* ............................... 81
Faro Shuffle* ...................................... 83
The Bridge* ........................................ 88
The Double Bridge* ............................. 90
*Really* Shuffle the Cards ..................... 93
False Cut* .......................................... 96

## CHAPTER 4
# CARDS AND CRAFTS

The Leap Frog ................................... 100
Cards in a Bottle ............................... 104
Playing Card Wallet ........................... 107
Post Card ......................................... 111
Marking Cards .................................. 113
Marked Miracle ................................ 117
Card Concealer .................................. 121

## CHAPTER 5
# CHEAP TRICKS

Fake Marked Cards* ........................... 126
Tearing a Deck in Half ....................... 129
Memorizing a Deck* ........................... 134
Getting Mental* ................................ 137
Back Breaker ..................................... 142

*\* = on companion DVD*

## CHAPTER 6
# WILD CARDS

Card Condo ....................................... 146
Card Calendar ................................... 150
Fortune-Telling ................................. 152
Card Box Balance ............................... 155
Card Ruler ........................................ 156
Card Calisthenics .............................. 158

## CHAPTER 7
# SAFE BETS

According to Hoyle ............................. 162
Three's a Crowd ................................ 166
Flipped* ........................................... 168
Joker Is on You! ................................ 172
Throwing Cards Into a Hat ................. 174
Stepping Through a Card .................... 176
Flicked ............................................. 180
Three-Card Monte (and the
    Bent Corner Ruse) .......................... 181

# LAST WORDS ...................................... 187

# APPENDIX

Further Reading ................................ 189
Acknowledgments .............................. 190
Credits ............................................. 191
Index ............................................... 196

# Foreword

**By David Blaine**

At the ripe age of 5, my mother gave me a strange gift. It was a deck of cards that her mother gave her. It immediately became my most prized possession and I never went anywhere without it. One day, a sweet librarian at the local Brooklyn library sat me down with a book of simple self-working card magic. Little did I know this would change my world forever. With just a deck of cards I had the ability to amaze anyone.

Joshua Jay was also introduced to playing cards at a young age. Since then, he has traveled the globe, cards in hand, and along the way has uncovered a wealth of information: shuffles, arcane playing card history, hilarious scams, and, of course, some amazing magic effects. I consider Josh an important emerging voice in our art. He is an incredible author, and I'm pleased that he has succeeded here—with this extraordinary celebration of cards, an easy-to-follow guide that will teach you some truly remarkable feats.

— DAVID BLAINE
*New York City*

The "Two Shoe" card shoe gives dealers the upper hand, *page 23.*

# Introduction

**Cards are power. Learn how to harness that power,
and you'll be forever rewarded.**

—James Swain, *21st Century Card Magic*

**P**laying cards is addictive. So are the playing cards themselves. My habit has me up to two packs a day. Next time you're in a bookstore, check out the gaming section. You'll notice several shelves packed tight with titles on card games, strategies, and "winning" formulas—all with outlandish claims of possessing the ultimate get-rich equation.

Now look down a shelf and to your right—after the crossword puzzles but before the role-playing games. You're in the section on magic tricks—a subject and art form I have studied and practiced continually since I was eight years old.

Between books about card games and magic manuals, there's an abyss. I've attempted to fill that void here. This book picks up after the card games stop and before the real magic tricks begin.

In the pages that follow, you'll learn card games you *can't* lose, exotic ways to shuffle, how to put a deck of cards in a glass bottle, the three-card monte hustle, astounding card miracles, calisthenics with cards, sleight of hand, how to morph a card prince into a frog, how to hide your valuables *in* a deck of cards, high-speed card throwing, how to memorize a deck in less than 10 seconds, and much more—in all, I give you 58 (one for every card in the deck, plus some bonus tricks for the jokers, and so on—there are actually 56 printed cards in every deck) fun and slightly strange uses for playing cards. You'll use them at work, at play, on your desk, and in the bar (after page 40, you'll never have to buy a drink again). But gambling isn't the only way to get hooked on cards. With a manageable amount of practice, you can become the local card whiz, whipping out fans and flourishes quicker than a gunslinger on the draw.

Some of the material in this book requires lots of practice to really make it look smooth. Other tricks can be done instantly, while you're reading. In all cases, I break down each technique into manageable, easy-to-learn actions, with photographs at every step.

I've got three suggestions for you as you carve your path to card awesomeness. First, learn the contents of this book in the order they appear. You can jump around if you want—I won't be offended. But the shuffling skills you learn in Chapter 1 will serve you well when you want to cheat at cards in Chapter 7 or dazzle your friends with tricks in Chapter 2. I've also rated the level of difficulty of each item, so you know what you're getting into. Stunts are rated 1 through 4 (represented visually by the four suits ♠♣♦♥), with level 1 being the most approachable—these are tricks or flourishes you can work instantly. A stunt rated 2 or 3 requires some practice. And a 4 might be more of an investment—it could take you three weeks of daily practice or longer to master. Seconds, minutes, hours, days—all spent with a deck of cards. Sounds like bliss to me.

Second, note the materials list—often you don't need more than a pack of cards, but pay attention to whether a crisp, new deck is warranted, or that old soft-edged deck will do. In some instances, a new deck will make an effect infinitely easier to perform.

Third, put this book down, pick up a pack of cards, and watch the accompanying 106-minute DVD we've included at the front of the book. This DVD features performances and tutorials for 29 tricks and stunts found in the book—plus one bonus effect that you won't find in these pages! I demonstrate some of my favorite magic effects, flashy flourishes, and bizarre shuffles, each one at performance speed; and then I teach the techniques. Use the DVD in conjunction with the book—if you're reading along and come to the DVD icon , cue up your disc and follow along with the tutorial—*or,* watch the DVD first, to inspire the basic moves, and then polish your techniques with the extra detail provided in the following pages.

Soon, a deck of cards will no longer be a way to pass the time; it might well become your way of life. Just grab a deck and keep reading.

# LET'S GET STARTED

**A** pack of cards has long been shrouded in mystery and deception. You're about to learn its secrets and how to dazzle people using just these 52 pieces of pasteboard (and maybe a couple jokers). Let's start with the first three lessons. Just answer this question first and then turn to page 4: How many of these nine cards are red?

*Continued*

# ∽ WELCOME BACK ∾

*continued from page 3*

There are five red cards, of course. I have no doubt you guessed that. But this question is misdirection, to conceal three other deceptions noted with callouts in the otherwise identical photo below:

Note that I asked you how many of the nine cards are red—but did you count the total or did you take my word for it? There are actually ten cards. Always make your opponents show you their hand. Always check twice. Always count. And always cut the cards.

And I'm sure you noticed that I'm holding the cards so you can see them. But did you notice that I was sporting an extra finger? That's sleight of hand, but with a fifth finger, it's most certainly not slight of hand. If you're trying to bust a cheat or solve a magic trick, heed this lesson: Cards only come to life when held between deft fingers. Pay closer attention to the hands than the cards.

Most surprising, I'll bet you didn't notice that the Ten of Hearts . . . is black! Even though the secret is right in front of our eyes, we don't see it because we aren't expecting it. Make no assumptions about playing cards.

There are 10 cards shown, not 9.

The Ten of Hearts is red!

Where did the extra finger come from?

# Playing Card Basics

**T**rying to learn the card stunts that follow without understanding the lingo would be like stepping into a hockey rink for a game without knowing how to skate (although here your teeth are not in jeopardy—not until the second chapter). Acquaint yourself with this basic terminology and form before proceeding:

**Dealers' Grip.** Hold the cards in your left hand, as if you were dealing cards for a game. The thumb rests along the left side, the index finger curls around the front of the deck, and the other finger pads rest on the right side.

NOTE: For ease of explanation, the stunts in this book are described for right-handed folks. If you're left-handed, simply reverse the actions.

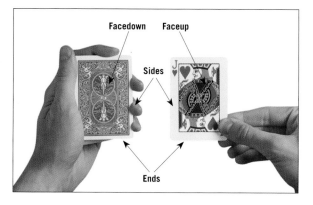

Facedown    Faceup

Sides

Ends

**The Parts of a Pasteboard.** Pasteboard is another term for playing cards, derived from a time when the front of a card was "pasted" onto its back. Here are some basic terms to know when handling a pack of pasteboards (otherwise known as a deck of cards).

Index

Pip

Index

**Index and Pip.** Several of the stunts described in this book require precise finger placement. The index portion is the part of the card with numbers or letters in the corner. Some European cards have four indices (one in each corner), but cards in the United States generally only have an index in the upper left and lower right. A pip is a suit symbol: A Six of Clubs has six Club "pips" (or eight, actually, if you count the two small symbols paired with the index).

Execute a card cascade, *page 33.*

# Chapter 1

# All Hands on Deck

. . . in shewing feats, and juggling with cards,
the principall point consisteth in shuffling them nimblie.

—Reginald Scot, *Discoverie of Witchcraft,* 1584

**R**eginald Scot, arguably the first English author to discuss uses for playing cards other than traditional card games, knew well the importance of handling a deck "nimblie."

Today we call this a "card flourish"—which is magicians' jargon for showing off. Magicians use flourishes to demonstrate dexterity. Most card flourishes look incredibly difficult because, well, they are. That being said, there are also a few smooth-as-silk moves that look master-level difficult but are in fact easy to learn and execute. Imagine the fear on your poker opponents' faces when they pull up their chairs around the table and see you fanning the deck with one hand, flipping the deck from one hand to the other, and casually cutting the cards one-handed.

# The Ribbon Spread and Flip

ON DVD

**MATERIALS: A new deck of playing cards, a soft but firm surface**    LEVEL: ♠ ♣ ♦ ♥

This flourish will wow any audience. Cards cascade from one side of the table to the other without you touching them! It's ideally performed on a firm but soft surface such as a tablecloth, carpeting, or a padded card table. Stay away from glass, Formica, or tiled tabletops, which cause the edges of the cards to slip.

**1.** Place the deck facedown on the left side of your work surface. Place your right hand on top of the tabled deck, gripping the pack by the ends between the thumb and fingers. Slide your first finger so it's positioned along the left side of the pack.

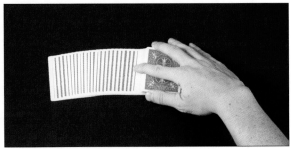

**2.** In one smooth action, smear the cards from left to right in a 20-inch spread, pressing gently along the side of the pack with your first finger to ensure the cards are distributed evenly. A quick, firm motion will encourage equal spacing between the cards (breaking tempo will cause the cards to clump and cluster). Practice the spread a dozen times before moving on to the next step; it's important your spread is even and straight.

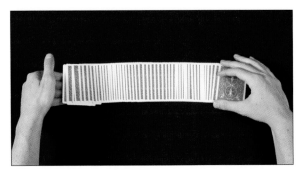

**3.** Position your left hand at the left side of the spread as you move your right hand to the right end of the spread. Maneuver the pads of the left fingers under the leftmost bottom card. (Alternatively, begin with your left fingers in this position in Step 1.)

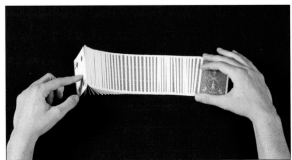

**4.** With the left fingers, carefully lift the left edge of the card, pivoting it up and to the right. Take care to leave the card's right side on the table.

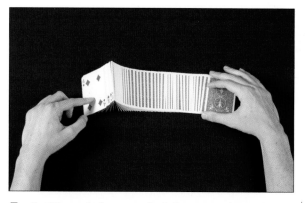

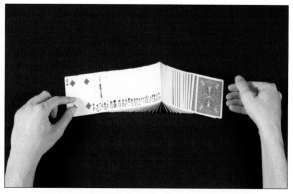

**5.** Swiftly push down on the leftmost card, causing the card to flip faceup.

**6.** In a chain reaction, the rest of the deck will also flip faceup, domino-style.

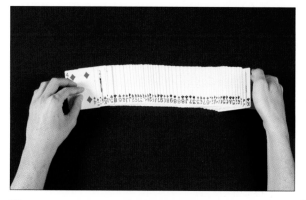

**7.** The slickest part of this flourish is that the right end of the deck flips faceup directly into the awaiting right fingers.

**8.** Now scoop the deck by sweeping with your right hand toward the left.

# One-Handed Flip

**MATERIALS: A new deck of playing cards, a soft but firm surface**     LEVEL: ♠ ♣ ♦ ♥

At this point, you probably think there's nothing more entertaining in the entire world than two-handed ribbon-spread flips (the Ribbon Spread and Flip, page 8). Wrong. Because you're about to do the same thing—but with one hand tied behind your back. I know, it's going to be mind-blowing.

**1.** Follow Steps 1 through 3 in the Ribbon Spread and Flip, page 8, sliding the first finger of your left hand under the leftmost card.

**2.** Slowly glide your finger across the edges of the cards in the ribbon spread, allowing your finger to fluidly "ride" the cards like a surfer rides a wave.

**3.** Practice maintaining this position while moving your finger back and forth along the length of the spread.

**4.** To finish the flourish, position your right hand to the right of the spread's center and release your grip from the cards. They will cascade domino-style, to the right side of the spread.

# No-Handed Flip

**MATERIALS: A new deck of playing cards, a soft but firm surface**     LEVEL: ♠ ♣ ♦ ♥

**I**n this variation, you cascade the deck of cards back and forth with ease. The tension of the deck is balanced on the edge of a single separate card. This action is referred to as "Walking the Dog."

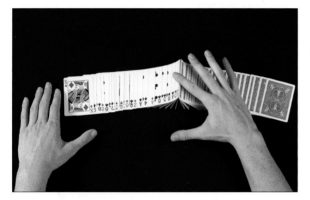

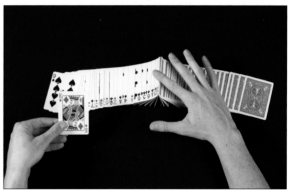

**1.** Follow Steps 1 through 3 in the Ribbon Spread and Flip, page 8, to begin with an evenly distributed ribbon spread. Initiate the flip at the leftmost point of the spread and allow the cards to glide along your right fingertip.

**2.** Since you are in the midst of the flip, the left side of the deck is faceup. With your left hand, pick up the leftmost card between your left thumb and fingers.

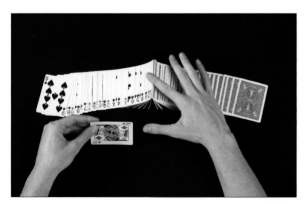

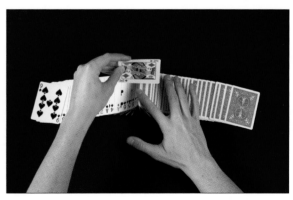

**3.** To transfer control of the ribbon spread from your right finger to the playing card in your left hand, hold the card in your left hand, perpendicular to the floor, so that you can see its face.

**4.** Balance the bottom edge of the card crosswise on the apex of the ribbon spread.

*Continued* ☞

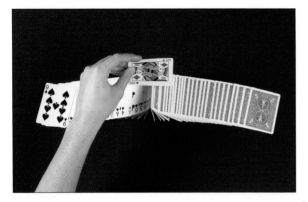

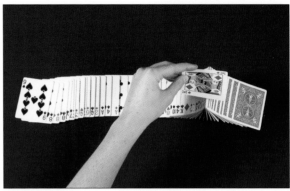

**5.** Slowly remove your finger, leaving the card edge in contact with the spread. The wave remains!

**6.** Move the left hand to the right and back to the left, all the while controlling the apex of the spread . . . without touching it directly.

## SLITHERING SNAKES AND SLICK SPREADS

David Hu, a Georgia Tech–based mechanical engineer and researcher, has made some groundbreaking discoveries about the way snakes move. And to communicate his findings, he compares a slithering snake to a ribbon spread deck of cards, just like the one described here.

Scientists previously attributed snake locomotion to pushing against obstacles like shrubs, plants, or rocks that lay in their paths. But Hu studied the motion of snakes on smooth surfaces, and came to a different conclusion. He discovered that the stomach scales on a snake overlap like "a spread of cards," which allows them to grip even a smooth surface to support the snake's body as it lifts itself up and forward. You can see precisely how this would work when you execute a ribbon spread: Examine how each overlapping card in the spread grips your working surface so it can bear the weight of the surrounding cards.

# No-Handed Flip Plus

ON DVD

**MATERIALS: A new deck of playing cards, a soft but firm surface**    LEVEL: ♠ ♣ ♦ ♥

**R**eady to take it to the next level? The No-Handed Flip Plus begins where the No-Handed Flip left off. While this isn't the most difficult flourish in the book, it *looks* that way, and that's enough to intimidate your Texas Hold 'Em opponents. If you've already mastered the No-Handed Flip, skip to Step 4.

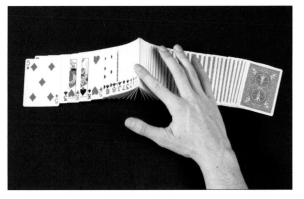

**1.** Begin in the starting position of a No-Handed Flip, page 11, with your right first fingertip gliding along the ribbon spread's apex.

**2.** Pick up the leftmost card between your left thumb and fingers.

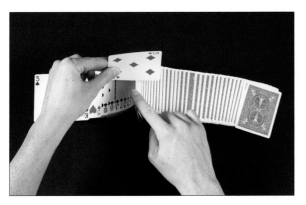

**3.** Transfer control of the ribbon spread from your right finger to the playing card in your left hand. Hold the card in your left hand, perpendicular to the floor.

**4.** While maintaining the spread's apex with the card in the left hand, grasp *another* card with your right hand, perhaps from the right end of the ribbon spread.

*Continued* ☞

**5.** Mirroring the actions of the left hand, position the card in your right hand on the apex of the spread, in the same place as the card in your left hand.

**6.** Simultaneously, move your hands in opposite directions. The left hand glides its card to the left as the right hand glides its card to the right. With a delicate touch, it will look like the photo above.

**7.** That is, you can *split* the apex, gliding half the spread to the left and the other half to the right. There. Now go practice your ribbon spreads.

## CARD QUIZ

**Is the Nine of Diamonds cursed?**

**Maybe.** Since the 18th century, the Nine of Diamonds has carried the nickname "the Curse of Scotland." The reason for this nickname is still debated by playing card historians. The stories possess the same "yeah right" element, but I prefer the grimmest theory. In 1692, Sir John Dalrymple contributed significantly to the Massacre of Glencoe, in which 38 Highland clansmen were killed. Dalrymple's coat of arms had nine diamondlike lozenges that are similar to the design on the Nine of Diamonds. Some contend that the order for the massacre was signed on the back of an actual Nine of Diamonds.

# Two-Handed Fan

ON DVD

**MATERIALS: *A new deck of playing cards***     **LEVEL:** ♠ ♣ ♦ ♡

**A** fan of cards is iconic. No, a fanned deck won't keep you cool on a hot day at the beach, but this flourish may make you look a little bit cooler in that bathing suit.

The key to this flourish is the condition of the pack. Forget about trying to fan your grandma's solitaire cards—after even minimal use, residue from your working surface collects on the cards, rendering them useless for tasks such as fanning and ribbon spreading. Brand-new cards, however, spread like butter.

**1.** Begin with the pack faceup, gripped from above in the right hand and from beneath in the left hand.

**2.** Place the inner left corner of the pack onto the webbing of the left thumb. You'll also note that the deck is situated in the left palm at an angle. This positioning will give the fan its symmetry later.

**3.** Extend your right first finger and place it on the left side of the pack, just below the outer left corner. The tip of the first finger should be at the same level as the lowermost card of the deck. The left thumb clamps down on the uppermost card of the pack.

*Continued* 👉

**4.** The first finger facilitates the fanning action. You'll move the finger in a clockwise, circular motion around the left hand, smearing the cards as you go. At the same time, the right first finger must move up slightly as it rotates, allowing its tip to graze every card during the action. The cards pivot under the left thumb, which remains in a clamped position.

**5.** If you end up with a large block of cards in an unspread condition on top of the pack, then you need to lift your right first finger more as you're fanning. Also, keep in mind that the left fingers play no part in the fanning action and remain stationary beneath the pack throughout. The cards in your fan should be evenly distributed, which is a result of a fast spreading action.

## CARD QUIZ

**Did each card always have an index in the corners?**

**Actually, no.** Before 1864, playing cards were only distinguishable by the suit pips across the face of the card. This required a card player to view every card completely to discern its value. Spreading cards this much made glimpsing an opponent's hand too easy.

An early solution to the problem, called "Triplicates," used a small picture of the entire card in the corners. Now a rare collector's item, Triplicate cards could be fanned tightly while allowing a player to see his entire hand of cards. Now, when you fan a deck of cards or hold a dealt hand between your fingers, you can easily see the values of all the cards, thanks to the indexes on each corner.

# Blank Fan

ON DVD

**MATERIALS: A deck of playing cards**          LEVEL: ♠ ♣ ♦ ♡

**W**hat do you do with a blank deck? Well, you can use it in an easy but impressive flourish that is especially effective with a borrowed deck, say before a game of cards—you can make any deck look like a trick deck. The identifying indices on playing cards are printed on the upper-left and lower-right corners (see diagram on page 5), which makes a traditional left-handed fan appear quite flashy. However, if you carry out the mechanics of a Two-Handed Fan with the deck in your right hand, not a single index is displayed except the one on the face of the deck.

**1.** Begin by cutting the Ace of Diamonds to the face of the deck. This card has the smallest area of ink on it, which makes it easy to disguise as a card without anything printed on it.

**2.** With the cards held in the *right* hand, execute a tight Two-Handed Fan (see page 15 for reference). No color should be visible. If any part of a card's suit is exposed, make tiny adjustments to the cards with the left fingers.

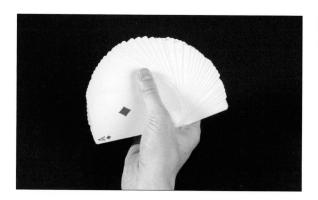

**3.** Place the right thumb pad on top of the Ace's outer right index, covering it from view.

*Continued* ☞

**4.** With the left thumb, cover the Diamond pip in the center of the card plus the inner right Ace index. You're holding the fan with two hands, which allows you to conceal the Ace of Diamonds. The result is a completely whitewashed pack!

## BLANK BACKS: A FAILED EXPERIMENT

It was a logical solution, so I can't blame them. Nineteenth-century card gaming was rife with cheating (on Mississippi riverboats, in tent-towns, at saloon games, and so on). Cards were marked (modified) by cheaters, and many card back designs were copied and printed with markings.

To combat these nefarious practices, card manufacturers instituted a bold solution: There would be no printing on card backs at all. The theory was that if there was no artwork to modify, any attempted marking would be obvious.

But cheats are as resourceful as they are greedy. Even though the backs appeared as blank (as in the Blank Fan taught here), cheats began marking the cards with dirt smudges. These tiny blemishes appeared to be nothing more than normal wear and tear, but to the informed cheat, the smudge was an easily identifiable mark. Cheats also developed a system for marking the *side* of each card. Called edgework, an unscrupulous player could nick the edge of all the high cards during play, and then sight these markings during subsequent rounds.

# Giant Fan

ON DVD

MATERIALS: **A deck of playing cards**     LEVEL: ♠ ♣ ♦ ♡

**I**f you're of the opinion that bigger is always better, then try this double-decker fan. It's an easy flourish to execute and the perfect way to impress your friends (and your enemies, too!) the next time you sit down at the card table.

**1.** Begin with the deck faceup as if you are about to deal cards in left dealing position.

**2.** With your left thumb, push the top card into the right hand.

**3.** Move the left hand forward and push the end of the second card until it protrudes halfway from the deck. In magic terminology, this is called "outjogging" a card.

**4.** Retract the left hand so it is once again even with the right, and push the third card over to the right hand. Outjog the fourth card and repeat this process with the rest of the deck. *Note:* Outjogging is admittedly tedious, and you can achieve the same results in seconds once you've mastered the Faro Shuffle (see page 83).

*Continued* ☞

**5.** When you've exhausted every card, gently square the sides of the elongated deck. The two packets should be interlaced (overlapped) about 1 inch.

**6.** Hold the packet that is closest to the body (the inner packet) in dealing grip, allowing the outer packet to protrude from the left hand.

**7.** Then spread the cards in a gentle arc between your left thumb and fingers . . .

**8.** . . . bracing the back of the fan from beneath with your right hand.

***Variation:*** For a more challenging move in Step 7, smear the right first finger in a clockwise motion.

Allow the left hand's cards to spread evenly, carrying out the same mechanics as a Two-Handed Fan (page 15).

Brace the spread at the area where the cards from both packets overlap.

## CARD QUIZ

**How big is the largest card fan?**

**The largest card fan included 326 cards, a world record held by Ralf Laue. On March 18, 1994, he held those 326 cards in a one-handed fan so that every index was visible.**

# One-Handed Fan

ON DVD

**MATERIALS: A new deck of playing cards**    LEVEL: ♠ ♣ ♦ ♥

**M**astering a sleight or flourish and then learning to do it with one hand is a recurring theme in this book, but keep these points in mind: First, flourishes with one hand look more impressive than two-handed stunts because they appear more difficult. Second, they often are more difficult—this item included. Third, think of all the cool things you can do with your other, free hand. You could scramble some eggs, play fetch with your dog, or hand out high fives!

The One-Handed Fan actually bears little resemblance to the Two-Handed Fan. The hand position is different, and the fanning action, this time performed with the left fingers, actually moves in a counterclockwise direction.

SIDE VIEW

**1.** The key to the One-Handed Fan lies in the starting position, so be precise with your grip. With your left hand, grip the pack (faceup) at the very end with the left thumb pad pressing against the uppermost card and running parallel along its end.

**2.** The left finger pads contact the lowermost card. Curl the left fingers and, like the left thumb, grip the pack at its very end.

**3.** Holding the left thumb relatively still, slowly straighten and extend the left fingers, causing the cards to spread and fan in a counterclockwise rotation.

**4.** As the fingers extend, the left thumb moves only slightly to the right, allowing the uppermost batch of cards to fan. The hardest part is getting the cards to curve around the hand. At first you'll find your One-Handed Fans almost linear in shape, but as you become more limber at uncurling your left fingers, the fans will gradually become more circular. Practice to develop a feel for the pressure you need to apply between your thumb and fingers: Your grip has to be firm enough to keep the cards held in a fanned position but loose enough to allow each card to spread.

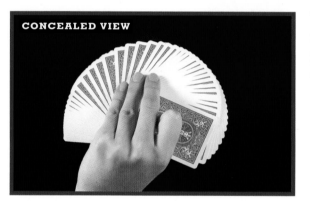

CONCEALED VIEW

**Variation:** As with the Two-Handed Fan (page 15), if you learn to fan the cards with your right hand, you'll have the added bonus of showing the deck blank (see Blank Fan, page 17).

## THE CARD SHOE BLUES

The card shoe is a gaming device, a version of which was devised by John Scarne, to prevent corrupt dealers from false dealing. But even the shoes themselves can be gaffed. The shoe depicted here is a rare "Two Shoe," named so because it can be used to deal the *second* card from the top. It also has a reflective, embedded prism near the top that divulges the identity of the top facedown, giving the dealer another unfair advantage.

# One-Handed Cut

**MATERIALS: A deck of playing cards**    **LEVEL:** ♠ ♣ ♦ ♥

"**C**ut 'em," your hotshot poker opponent says as he drops the deck on the table. Who is this guy, and why is he using that tone with you? No biggie. You pick up the cards, yawn, and cut them with one hand. He swallows hard. This is called intimidation. For best results, you have to *play down* these flourishes; they should look effortless.

Actually, the cut is called the Charlier (Shar-lee-ay) cut and was invented more than a hundred years ago by a French guy named . . . Charlier (just one name—think Madonna or Sting).

**1.** You'll need only one hand for this cut, so put your nondominant hand somewhere out of the way. Begin by holding the cards facedown in your dominant hand, using your thumb pad to support one side of the pack and your finger pads to grip the opposite side. Grip the deck at the very tips of the fingers, allowing for maximum space beneath the cards and your palm.

**2.** Bend your thumb slightly, easing your grip on the sides of the cards. Allow approximately half of the cards in the deck to drop down from the thumb onto the palm like it's hinged.

**3.** Curl your first finger and move it below the dropped packet.

**4.** Push up on the underside of the packet with the first finger.

**5.** When the lower half of the deck clears the upper packet, let the upper packet fall . . .

**6.** . . . followed in quick succession by the second. (Release the thumb's grip on the cards, and both packets will collapse into your palm.)

## CARD QUIZ

**Where do playing cards come from?**

**Playing cards are thought to have originated in central Asia during the 10th century. They looked like flattened dominoes and were used for game play.**

Playing cards spread through Persia to Egypt. In Egypt, the Mamluk people developed four suits for their cards: swords, polo sticks, cups, and coins, which represented aspects of daily life for Mamluk aristocracy. Four-suited cards reached the European gentry around 1370. These hand-painted cards were used for game play as well, but reserved mostly for royalty. Soldiers carried playing cards across the warpaths of Europe to England and France.

The French gave playing cards an overhaul, dressing the figures in 15th-century royal garb, and categorizing the cards into the four suits we use today: *Pique* (Spade), *Carreau* (Diamond), *Trèfle* (Club), and *Coeur* (Heart).

Five colorful court cards from 16th-century Rouen, France, illustrate the original royal dress.

# Self-Cutting Deck

**MATERIALS: A deck of playing cards, a bed or a chair**     LEVEL: ♠ ♣ ♦ ♥

**Y**ou could classify this as both a trick and a flourish. Either way, it's cool to see it work. But follow these instructions carefully, or you'll find yourself playing 52-card pickup. Here's the effect: Holding a deck of cards, extend your hand and ask someone to cut the cards. Just before his hand reaches the pasteboards, half the cards fly out of your left hand and into your awaiting right fingers—the deck cuts itself!

**1.** Hold the deck facedown, gripped between the thumb and finger pads of your left hand, in an elevated position. Curl the left first finger around the front end of the pack. *Tip:* Sit to practice this effect (it's far easier to gather cards from your lap than from the floor).

**2.** Extend your hand toward the card opponent or participant nearest you and ask him to cut the cards. Inconspicuously move the right hand between the left hand and your body in preparation for catching the lower half of the deck.

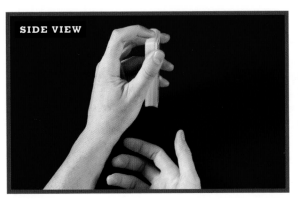

**3.** With your left first finger, gently contact the outer end of the pack.

**4.** Jerk your left first finger inward toward your body, projecting the lower portion of the deck into the palm of your right hand.

**5.** Catch the packet in the right hand and without pausing . . .

**6.** . . . place the packet on top of the cards in the left hand. This move is all attitude and timing. Think James Bond. The timing is like this: "Would you cut the cards?" Pause one beat, then execute the move. "Thanks, that's perfect."

## CARD QUIZ

**Where did the expression "Not playing with a full deck" come from?**

**England, 1707.** Queen Anne enforced a tax on playing cards that eventually affected both manufacturers and the public (this practice continued in the U.K. until 1960). In 1828, manufacturers placed the tax stamp on the Ace of Spades instead of the box. These stamps were taken seriously by the English government: One Richard Hardy was *executed* for forging such a stamped Ace. To avoid paying the inflated price, some English citizens began to purchase decks without any Aces of Spades. Hence they were "playing without a full deck."

# Catch-a-Deck

**MATERIALS: A deck of worn-in playing cards, the card box, edge of a table**

**LEVEL: ♠ ♣ ♦ ♥**

This is another impressive stunt in which you apparently catch an entire deck of cards in midair. Until you have practiced the mechanics a few times, keep the deck in its box. The case will function as training wheels, preventing you from dropping the cards everywhere or scraping a knee.

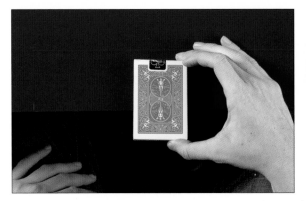

**1.** Rest the deck (or filled card box) on the edge of the table so that approximately half protrudes over the edge.

**2.** Carefully position the backs of the right first, second, third, and fourth fingers under the protruding deck or box. Extend the thumb about three inches below the fingers, preparing to catch the cards.

**3.** In one fluid motion, quickly raise the right hand and jerk it forward with a cobralike movement. The fingers cause the deck to rotate end-to-end 180 degrees . . .

**4.** . . . and then stop, securely pinned between the thumb and fingers.

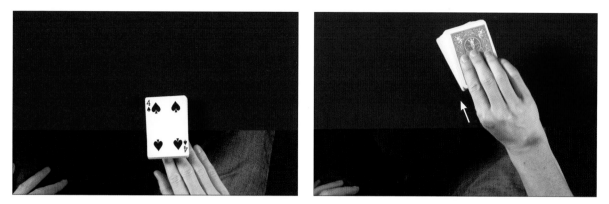

**5.** If you haven't already, remove the box. When you're hitting this stunt consistently, be brave and slide the cards from the box. The handling is exactly the same; the cards will remain as a unit during their brief flight.

*Variation:* Once you've got the stunt down without the box, try catching the deck blindfolded.

## SLEIGHTS WITHOUT SIGHT

If you think the stunts in this book are difficult, imagine learning and performing *without looking.* Richard Turner is considered to be one of the finest card handlers in the world; Richard Turner is also blind. Turner's deft manipulations have helped him achieve an unparalleled finger sensitivity. He can *feel* the difference between red and blue cards: "The red ink is cakier," he says. His skill has led the U.S. Playing Card Company to hire Turner as a quality-control consultant.

I went on a pilgrimage to meet and share card tricks with Richard Turner. After he amazed me with his sleight of hand, it was my turn to perform. But how does someone who cannot see watch a magic effect? He placed his hands on mine and felt my sleight of hand, which allowed him to visualize the tricks I performed.

# Throwing Cards

**MATERIALS: *Several new playing cards***    **LEVEL:** ♠ ♣ ◆ ♥

Thrown playing cards *can* be used for self-defense. Historically, scaling (another term for throwing) cards has almost always been reserved for a display of skill. Howard Thurston, America's foremost magician at the beginning of the nineteenth century (see box, page 32), was known to scale hundreds of promotional cards into the audience at incredible speeds and distances—even into theater balconies.

Whether you're defending a damsel in distress or just have a desire to throw something fast enough to leave a mark, scaling a playing card is easier than it looks. Just make sure you aim away from innocent bystanders: Even playing cards can draw blood!

**1.** Begin by holding a playing card in your right hand. Rest the pad of your first finger on the edge of the outer left corner while you pinch the card between the thumb from above and the second finger from beneath.

# CARD QUIZ

**What is the farthest distance a playing card has ever been thrown?**

In the 1970s, expert sleight-of-hand artist Ricky Jay set world records for his card-throwing skills. Today, magician Rick Smith holds the world record. Smith used to be a pitcher at Cleveland State University, and perhaps it was this training that helped earn him the world's record: 216' 4" (at 92 miles per hour).

**2.** Curl your right hand in toward your body and flick the card forcefully, parallel with the ground, as you would throw a Frisbee.

**3.** The card must rotate off the first finger. If the card flutters to the ground just inches from your body, you either aren't getting enough rotation during the release or you're throwing the card at an angle (always aim to toss the card parallel with the ground).

**4.** Once you've got a working formula for throwing the card, practice increasing the force of your throw: Specifically, use more arm strength and focus on "snapping" the wrist as you release the card. Gym-goers, remember snapping towels in the locker room? Same move. When you scale a card properly, you'll know it. The card will whiz by at a speed disproportionate to the amount of force you applied.

# A SCALING LEGEND

**H**oward Thurston (1869–1936) was one of magic's brightest lights during the vaudeville era. He toured with an enormous illusion show, yet one of his most enduring stunts was card-throwing. Thurston printed special cards with his likeness (and sometimes advertising on the verso), which he would scale into the audience. He was reported to have incredible accuracy, and could even reach the back row of theater balconies.

# Card Cascade

**MATERIALS: A deck of playing cards**     **LEVEL:** ♠ ♣ ♦ ♥

In this elegant and classic flourish, you cascade an entire deck of cards from one hand to the other. The cards fall so smoothly and fast that they appear to behave like liquid: Indeed, this flourish is sometimes referred to as the Waterfall. Be warned, Card Cascade will take considerable time to master, so patience, as always, is key.

**1.** Hold the deck at the ends between your right thumb and finger pads. Hold the inner edge of the pack against the base of the thumb pad, as shown.

**2.** Straighten your fingers while you squeeze the pack, applying pressure near the top cards between your thumb and fingers and successively less pressure at the face of the deck.

*Continued* ☞

## SHOW-OFF

Magic is the art of concealing art. If a magician's technique is perceived or even suspected, the illusion of impossibility is shattered. This is why many magicians who possess extraordinary skill with playing cards elect not to perform fancy shuffles, fans, and flourishes in their acts. Instead, magicians simulate normal card handling—neat but not flashy—and perform their sleights with stealth, dexterity, and ultra-smoothness.

So what purpose do these flourishes serve? They are wonderful exercises to increase finger strength and agility. And they look *so cool*.

**3.** By squeezing the pack in this fashion, you inflate the deck at the center to nearly twice its thickness.

**4.** Lift your right hand to chest height, holding the deck perpendicular to the floor. Position your left hand beneath the right, palm up and outstretched, ready to catch falling cards. At first, keep your hands relatively close together: Six inches is a good starting distance. (As you become more proficient, widen the space between your hands to more than 15 inches.)

## CARD QUIZ

**How can the cascade be so perfect in those photos of magicians?**

**We cheat.** Many magicians use a prop called an Electric Deck. This is a specialty pack sewn together loosely that allows you to simulate a cascade without any real manipulation.

**5.** Gently release your grip on the cards at the face of the deck. They will begin to fall, in quick succession, from the face toward your left palm. As you ease your grip, cards nearer the top will continue to fall.

**6.** Release your grip completely, allowing the last cards to fall from your right hand to the left. The entire cascade should last no more than three seconds, and no cards should change order. This flourish is always accompanied by an audible *frrrrrrrrrrrp* as the cards fall. If you experience cards falling in clumps or all at once, use a newer pack. If the problem persists, concentrate on practicing a fluid release of pressure from the bottom to the top.

# The Ultimate Catch

**MATERIALS: A deck of playing cards**     LEVEL: ♠ ♣ ♦ ♥

This stunt is the most difficult one in the book and will take considerable time to master. I recommend practicing it while seated on the floor so you're closer to the cards when they fall . . . and they *will* fall. But once you're an expert, spreading a pack along the length of your arm, flipping it, throwing the cards upward, and snatching the entire spread from the air, jaws—not cards—will drop to the floor.

**1.** Straighten your wrist and hold your left forearm perfectly horizontal, parallel to the ground. Face your left palm upward.

**2.** With your right hand, spread the pack from the palm of your left hand to your elbow. Keep the cards evenly spaced and as straight as possible.

**3.** Using your left fingers, lever the bottom cards of the deck over to trigger the Flip (see page 8).

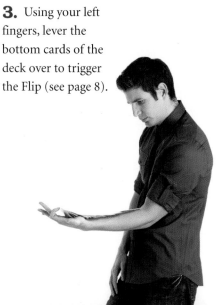

**4.** With your right fingers, guide the apex of the Flip toward your left elbow. Keep your left hand perfectly flat and still, or you risk dropping cards.

**5.** Insert your right thumb beneath the top card of the deck at your elbow as it flips over. Hover your right fingers above the pack, in preparation to "scoop" them from midair.

**6.** Quickly jerk your left forearm upward, propelling the cards into the air. Try to toss them so the spread remains evenly spaced in its trajectory.

**7.** In a quick forward motion, collect the airborne cards, snatching them with your right thumb and fingers.

**8.** And don't forget to follow through!

Sleight of hand card magic has existed almost as long as cards themselves.

# Chapter 2

# Tricks

**"Do you like card tricks?" he asked.**

**"No, I hate card tricks," I answered.**

**"Well, I'll just show you this one."**

**He showed me three.**

—W. SOMERSET MAUGHAM, *Mr. Know All*

**"Do you like card tricks?" he asked.**

**I said no. He asked me if I liked knees to my groin. I said no.**

**He said, "Then take a card."**

—STEVE BEAM, *Semi-Automatic Card Tricks, Volume 2*

Card magic is not only the ultimate party trick, it's an excellent way to bring friends together, entertain family, or break the ice with new people. Some card tricks take

a lifetime to perfect, but the effects in this chapter—all of professional caliber—can be mastered almost instantly.

As trick editor for *MAGIC* magazine, dozens of amazing card tricks appear in my mailbox every day. I've taken some of the best ideas from this publication and from the history of the art and made them

self-working. I've also given you a variety of effects, which will allow you to combine tricks and perform your own close-up show. This material is perfect for first dates, poker breaks, or wowing friends. A professional magician could earn a living with the card tricks described in this chapter. Try them as you read; you might even fool yourself.

# The Card Shark

**ON DVD**

**MATERIALS: A deck of playing cards**     **LEVEL:** ♠ ♣ ♦ ♥

**A**s if finding a spectator's card in the deck weren't enough, you also manage to produce a royal flush in Spades. *Warning:* Nobody will play cards with you after seeing this trick, so choose your marks wisely.

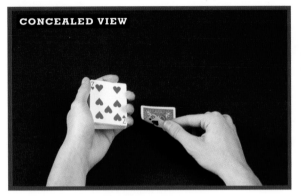

**CONCEALED VIEW**

**1.** Pull the Ten of Spades from the deck and place it facedown on the table.

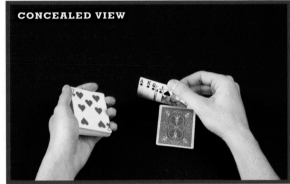

**CONCEALED VIEW**

**2.** Place the Jack of Spades facedown on top, followed by the Queen, King, and Ace of Spades.

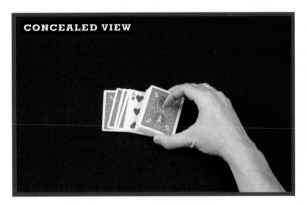

**CONCEALED VIEW**

**3.** Next, place any Six, say the Six of Hearts, faceup on top of the pile. Place the rest of the deck facedown on top, and you're ready to begin. *Optional:* If you're feeling saucy, throw in a False Cut (see page 96).

**4.** Place the deck facedown on the table, saying, "I'll show you why you should never play cards with me."

**5.** Ask the participant to cut the cards, and place the cut-off packet on the table.

**6.** Ask her to remember the card she cut to, pointing to the card on top of the lower portion of the deck. Let's say this card is the Seven of Clubs.

**7.** Instruct her to place this card on top of the pile already in front of her (the original top half of the deck) . . .

**8.** . . . and complete the cut. While it appears that this process has hopelessly buried the participant's card, it has actually been positioned exactly six cards below the faceup Six.

*Continued* ☞

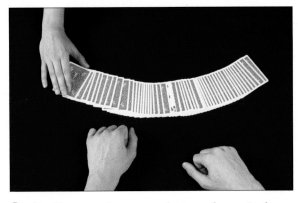

**9.** "I will now make your card appear faceup in the deck." Snap your fingers, shake your groove thing, or perform any gesture that could be construed as magic. Ask the participant to spread the deck facedown across the table. This will reveal the faceup Six of Hearts. To the spectator, this is unimpressive, as it appears your trick has failed.

**10.** Separate the deck at the faceup card, making the Six of Hearts the top card of the lower half of the spread. Square this portion of cards into a pile and hand it to the participant.

**11.** Feigning disappointment, ask, "You didn't pick the Six?" Appear to gather your thoughts. "I knew that. The Six is an indicator card; it's sending us a message. Why don't you count down six cards." Take the Six from the top of the participant's pile and display it. Instruct the participant to deal six cards onto your outstretched left hand.

**12.** As she deals the sixth card, ask her what card she selected (the Seven of Clubs). Instruct her to turn over the sixth card . . . the Seven of Clubs is revealed!

**13.** She's amazed. "But," you say, "that isn't the reason why you should never play cards with me...." Draw attention to the five facedown cards she just dealt onto your hand. "*This* is why you should never play cards with me!" Dramatically reveal the contents of your hand: a royal flush in Spades.

## CARD SHARPS AND CARD SHARKS

Card sharpers and card sharks both refer to nefarious gamblers. The term "sharper" (as in a player who is *sharper* than his opponents) first appeared in 1681, while the term "shark" was first used in a cheating context in 1599. Bottom line: For poker safety, avoid sharp objects and don't swim with sharks.

## CARD QUIZ

**How are playing cards made?**

**They're actually layered.** Standard playing cards are composed of three layers made from fiber rags mixed with a china clay (the clay gives the pulp its white coloring). An adhesive made with carbon black is used to glue the pieces together; this adhesive adds to the opacity of each card. Casein and borax coatings are applied to the front and back, and this finish gives the cards their slick feel. Playing cards are printed on large sheets, which are then punched out for assembly and packaging.

# One Ahead

ON DVD

**MATERIALS: A deck of playing cards**          **LEVEL:** ♠ ♣ ♦ ♥

This card trick, one of the oldest (and best) in the world, will come naturally to good poker players or great liars.

Oh, good, you're still here.

Magicians call this the one-ahead principle because you begin with prior knowledge of one of the three cards. In this way you can predict all three cards; but the *order* of the cards is a total bluff.

**1.** Ask someone to shuffle a deck thoroughly, and as they shuffle, secretly sight the top card of the deck. (*Note:* Sometimes this is easy; sometimes it's impossible.) Remember it. Let's assume it's the Three of Clubs.

If you can't see the top card during the participant's shuffle, glimpse the one on the bottom. This card is much easier to see.

**2.** Stress the fact that the participant has done all the shuffling and that you haven't touched the cards. Ask her to cut the deck into three piles.

**3.** Pay attention to where the glimpsed card (Three of Clubs) resides as the participant cuts. It will usually be on the left or the right, depending on whether you remembered the top or bottom card, and whether your participant cut right to left or left to right. It doesn't make any difference—you just have to secretly note where it is. Let's assume the Three of Clubs is on top of the rightmost pile.

**4.** "Despite your shuffling," you say, "I'm going to ascertain three cards by osmosis." So saying, place your first finger on the top card of the leftmost pile. (At this point you must always place your finger on a pile *other than* the one with the remembered card.) Close your eyes and concentrate, as if learning the identity of the card through your fingertips. Then proclaim, "This one is the Three of Clubs!"

**5.** Pick up that top card from this pile and hold it toward yourself in your left hand the way you would hold cards during a game. It's important that nobody else can see this card, and that you note the identity of this card. Let's say it's the King of Hearts. Even though this card is not the Three of Clubs (and you claimed it was), smile like you got it right.

*Continued*

**6.** Place a finger on the other pile without the Three of Clubs (in our case this would be the middle pile). "This feels like the King of Hearts!" you say.

**7.** Pick up the card off the center pile and place it next to the card in your left hand. Casually notice its value; perhaps it's the Five of Spades. Again, act content with your guess.

**8.** Now put your finger on the last pile. Even though you know which card is on top (Three of Clubs), you must miscall this card. Call out the name of the card you just picked up from pile 2. "This last one I'm not sure about, but I'm pretty sure it's the Five of Spades."

**9.** Pick up the top card of the last pile with your right hand and transfer it *to the face of* the pair of cards in your left hand.

**10.** "I'll bet you don't believe me. See?" So saying, lower your hand so the participant can see the value of the cards.

**11.** Thumb over the top faceup card (the Three of Clubs) onto the left pile.

**12.** Then, in a continuing action, deal the King of Hearts onto the center pile, and finally drop the Five of Spades onto the last pile. Three cards by osmosis!

## CARD QUIZ

**How many decks of cards are printed each year?**

**Millions.** In the United States alone, approximately 150 million packs are printed every year. That's nearly one deck for half the people in America!

# The Ten-Twenty Force

**MATERIALS: A deck of playing cards, a scrap of paper**     **LEVEL:** ♠ ♣ ♦ ♥

"**P**ick a card, any card." You've heard that before. But have you heard the term "force"? Magicians often influence a person's choice and make someone take a predetermined card, which is called a card force. Now don't be alarmed, but my guess is that some of you may not have actually had a free choice the last time you picked a card from a magician. You're about to learn a classic card force. And all you need to be able to do is count and/or add to 20 to do it. So, without further ado, for all you math whizzes still with me . . .

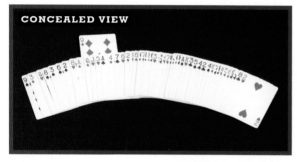

CONCEALED VIEW

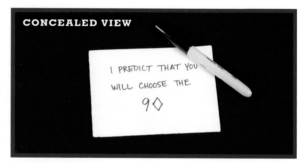

CONCEALED VIEW

**1.** Set the card you wish to force, say the Nine of Diamonds, at the 10th position from the top of the deck of cards.

**2.** Then write the following prediction on a scrap of paper: "I predict that you will choose the Nine of Diamonds." Fold the prediction in quarters.

**3.** When you're ready to perform, introduce your folded prediction and ask someone to hold it, instructing her not to read it yet.

**4.** Ask that participant to think of any number between 10 and 20 (let's say she chooses 14), and have her deal that many cards facedown into a pile on the table. Instruct her to set the remainder of the deck aside.

**5.** Turn your back (so you can't see) and ask her to pick up the smaller packet of cards. Have her add the two digits of her chosen number to get a new number. (*Example:* If she originally counted 14 cards on the table, then she adds 1 plus 4 to get 5.)

**6.** With your back still turned, ask the participant to deal from the packet the number of cards equal to the sum of the digits into a new pile. Instruct her to flip over and look at the card that falls on this number. It will be, in this case, the Nine of Diamonds. This will work every time so long as your force card is in the 10th position and your spectator can add.

**7.** The force is only half the presentation. Now you "sell" the miracle—like this: "So let's recap. You thought of any number and, without telling me, you dealt that many cards. Then you formed a new number. Again, I have no idea what this number is or what your original number was. You now have a card in your mind, and you haven't told anyone the name of that card, right?" She agrees.

**8.** Then you direct her to the folded prediction in her hand: "For the first time, read the prediction that you've been holding since *before* you thought of your card."

You know, they used to burn witches for stunts less powerful . . .

# Finding Four Aces Without Touching the Deck

**MATERIALS: A deck of playing cards**      **LEVEL:** ♠ ♣ ♦ ♥

**Y**ou've heard of magicians cutting to four Aces, right? Well, that's a pretty good trick, but it's not perfect. The reason it isn't perfect is because the magician has to touch the cards to cut four Aces. In this trick, you can cut to four Aces without even touching the cards! It's almost otherworldly. As soldier Richard Middleton said in the late 17th or early 18th century, "The Ace is the only God." (He was caught playing with cards in church.) Centuries later, many card sharks would likely agree.

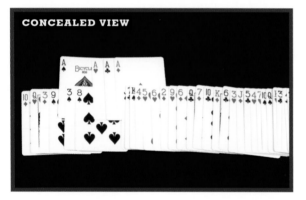

**1.** Secretly stack the deck in advance. From the top down, order the cards like this: any four indifferent cards, Ace of Spades, two indifferent cards, Ace of Hearts, Ace of Clubs, Ace of Diamonds, then the rest of the deck.

**2.** Forget that the cards are stacked, and hand the deck to a participant. (*Optional:* You may throw in a False Cut [page 96], to give the appearance of a mixed pack.) Tell her, "You'll be my hands, eyes, and brain, but I'll still locate all four Aces." Then prompt her to "Think of any number between, say, 10 and 20. Got it? This is your secret number."

**3.** Instruct the participant to count down to her secret number, counting one card for each number into a facedown pile. You can even turn your back so you won't see how many cards she's counted. You ask, "Have you done that? Great. Place the rest of the deck aside."

**4.** Instruct the participant to hold the small pile of dealt cards. You say, "We're going to find the first Ace with a new number. To determine what your new number is, add the two single digits of your secret number together." For instance, if her secret number is 17, she will add 1 plus 7 to get a new number, 8 in this case. Instruct her to deal a pile of facedown cards, one at a time, equal to her new number.

**5.** The card that falls on this new number—which you determined by your own whim—should be the first Ace. Accordingly, you announce, "The Ace of Diamonds? Perfect."

**6.** Now you work it, reminding the participant that she's in control. You say, "Since I couldn't possibly know which number you were thinking of, I certainly don't know the new one. I also haven't a clue how many cards are on the table, how many are left in the packet, or how many are left in your hand. Obviously, then, I have no idea what the identity of any of those cards is either. Still," you announce, "we're going to find the other Aces. And we'll find them using a spell—or more precisely, spelling."

*Continued* ☞

**7.** Make sure your participant is still holding the packet facedown in her hand, and ask her to envision the Ace of Hearts. "Now you'll cast a spell, actually spelling the name of this Ace, one card for each letter." Ask her to transfer a card from the top of the packet to the bottom for each letter in Ace of Hearts (A-C-E-O-F-H-E-A-R-T-S). She should transfer one card from top to bottom for A, then another for C, one for E, then another for O, and so on.

**8.** Ask her to turn over the card she's holding on the last letter, S. It will be the Ace of Hearts! "There," you say, "I've found a second Ace without even touching the cards."

**9.** "Now," you say, "let's try that again: This time spell Ace of Spades, one card for each letter." She spells out A-C-E-O-F-S-P-A-D-E-S. When she flips over the last S card, it's the Ace of Spades. "You say it worked again?" you brag. "I *told* you I could find the Aces without touching the cards!" Three down, one to go.

**10.** You've successfully located the Ace of Diamonds, Ace of Hearts, and Ace of Spades. "What's left?" you ask. Your participant answers, "The Ace of Clubs?" "Right!" you answer, excited. "Now spell 'right'—R-I-G-H-T." She counts out the next five cards and looks at the last one in her hand . . . and you're right! You've located (with your participant's help) the Ace of Clubs.

**11.** Ta-da! Four Aces without ever touching the cards. *Note:* If you place the cards in the order explained in Step 1, the trick is automatic. The first Ace is located with the Ten-Twenty Force, which you already know (page 48). What's interesting about its application here is that besides forcing the 10th card, it also situates exactly nine cards in the participant's hand. I discovered that these nine cards can be prearranged and that the force maintains their sequence.

**Variation:** You can vary the ending to suit the situation. I like to spell "R-I-G-H-T" because it sounds casual and gets a laugh. If you prefer, you can spell any other five-letter word appropriate for the trick: M-A-G-I-C, C-L-U-B-S, or even a participant's name, provided you know in advance that his or her name is spelled with five letters.

## CARD QUIZ

**Are some playing cards valuable?**

**Yes.** The most expensive deck of playing cards was sold at auction in Sotheby's, London, in 1983. The Metropolitan Museum of Art in New York City purchased a vintage deck of cards, hand-painted around 1470. It is believed to be the oldest complete deck of cards in existence. They paid $143,352.

## CARD QUIZ

**What is the Solitaire Encryption Algorithm (and is it part of our homework)?**

---

**Bruce Schneier developed a system of coding messages using a deck of 52 playing cards and two Jokers, which he calls the "Solitaire Encryption Algorithm" (Solitaire).** Using a deck of playing cards as an encryption method is ideal, because cards seem so ordinary. Computers, crib sheets, and decoders are all incriminating evidence should the secret police break down your front door. On the other hand, anyone could (and, in my opinion, *should*) have a deck of cards handy. And when they arrive at your door, the evidence is lost with a shuffle of the cards.

This isn't some simple encryption that works in conjunction with a plastic decoder ring. "Solitaire" is designed to deceive military opposition, top cryptanalysts, and the world's most complex computers. Schneier even takes into account that adversaries may be familiar with "Solitaire," but since part of the code pivots on the random result of a shuffled deck, it is almost impossible to decipher.

Other, simpler codes exist with a pack of cards. If your message is short, write it on the edges of a shuffled deck (below). Write down the order of the cards; this will be your key. Now shuffle the cards. Only someone with the key order will be able to read your message.

# Pointer Power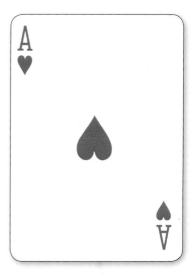

**MATERIALS: A deck of playing cards**      LEVEL: ♠ ♣ ♦ ♥

**F**or obvious reasons, it doesn't seem that cards marked secretly on their *faces* would be of much use. But, you'll use an old magician's marking system on the face of certain playing cards to determine a chosen card.

Certain cards are known as "pointer" cards. By its design, the orientation on a pointer card is easily distinguishable from other cards—it "points." As an example, remove the Ace of Hearts. Orient the card so that the point of the heart is away from you. This card is now "pointing" up. If you rotate the card 180 degrees, the heart will appear upright, pointing in the opposite direction. This is only true of certain cards. The Two of Spades or Ace of Diamonds, for instance, cannot be distinguished upside down or right-side-up due to their symmetry.

**1.** Remove an assortment of about six pointer cards. Any pointer cards will work, but try to get a balance of colors, values, and suits. Here is the assortment I like to use: Ace of Hearts, Three of Spades (two of the Spades point in the same direction), Five of Hearts (the center Heart pip indicates which way the card points), Five of Clubs (works the same as the Five of Hearts), Nine of Spades (the center Spade pip is directional), and the Seven of Diamonds (the center Diamond pip always favors one end). Here, all six cards point in the same direction (up, or toward the participant).

*Continued* ☞

**2.** Give your packet a thorough overhand shuffle. If you're feeling bold, you can even ask a spectator to shuffle, miming the actions of an overhand mix. Because the packet is so small, it is unlikely that she will turn cards end for end during the shuffle. The direction of the cards will be maintained.

**3.** Spread the cards facedown between your hands and ask her to take one from the spread. Let's say she chooses the Seven of Diamonds.

**4.** Close the spread and say, "I'll turn away so you can look at your card and show it to everybody else." When you turn your back, secretly rotate your packet 180 degrees so it is pointing in the opposite direction.

**5.** Spread the cards between your hands again and ask the spectator to insert her card back into the spread. Then execute an overhand shuffle (or invite her to shuffle) once more.

**6.** Flip the packet faceup and thumb through the cards one by one, with a pensive look on your face.

**7.** One card will be pointing in the opposite direction (in this case, the Seven of Diamonds) . . . her selection.

## CARD QUIZ

**Can you make explosives with playing cards?**

**Perhaps once upon a time.** Decades ago, back when playing cards were made with paper, the red ink on the cards contained diazo dye, which when combined with certain other materials was said to make an explosion.

Author Tom Robbins explains the recipe for a homemade playing card "pow" in *Still Life with Woodpecker.* Moisten and tear up the Hearts and Diamonds until they're mush, and then stuff them into a pipe, plugged at one end. Mix the suits with a household product high in glycerin (Robbins suggests hand lotion) and add potassium permanganate (found in the snakebite section of the first-aid kit under the sink). Plug the pipe and light the thingy on fire. It will explode, shooting a fiery wad out of the end of the pipe!

But cards today aren't explosive as they once were—and tearing up a handful of hearts and diamonds will only succeed in ruining a perfectly good deck of cards!

# Barely Lift a Finger

ON DVD

**MATERIALS: A deck of playing cards, a thin rubber band**     **LEVEL:** ♠ ♣ ♦ ♥

I showed you how to find four Aces without even touching the deck (page 50), but that method requires spelling, which may challenge some people (I'm not judging). In this method, you locate all four Aces simultaneously simply by lifting your finger. Best of all, it takes no skills, spelling or otherwise.

**CONCEALED VIEW**

**1.** In preparation, remove the four Aces and wrap a rubber band around the rest of the deck.

**CONCEALED VIEW**

**2.** Place the Aces on the face of the pack, beneath the wrapped deck. This does require an audience assumption that you begin with a rubber band around the deck.

**3.** As long as you hold the deck in a Dealers' Grip, the pack will look like it is enveloped by the rubber band.

**4.** Explain that you will find all four Aces by simply lifting a finger. As you talk, move the right fingers over the deck and grip the upper half by the ends.

**5.** Lift the upper half of the cards up and to the right, while still under the wrapped band.

**6.** Rotate the right hand clockwise, turning the upper packet, causing the rubber band to twist. The upper packet should now be faceup and the rubber band should be tight.

**7.** Fold the right hand's packet *beneath* the left-hand packet of cards.

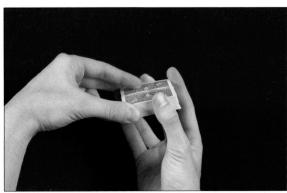

**8.** Take care to keep the deck square at this point; you don't want to locate the hidden Aces prematurely.

*Continued* 👉

CONCEALED VIEW

**9.** By cutting the cards in this way, you have tucked the four "unbanded" Aces in the center of an otherwise banded deck.

**10.** Carefully place the banded deck on the table, all the while keeping the cards square. Readjust so that your right first finger is pressed on top of the deck firmly, keeping all the other cards in alignment.

**11.** Now for the easy part: locating four Aces by simply lifting a finger. Lift your finger. When you release, the top packet should spin, leaving four cards protruding from the center of the deck.

**12.** Dramatically remove these cards and display the four Aces to your audience.

*Variation:* For another spectacular reveal, hide the Aces faceup in Step 2.

# BRAILLE PLAYING CARDS

agician Whit Haydn once approached a table to perform restaurant magic for a little girl and her parents. It quickly became apparent that she was blind and unable to enjoy card tricks in the conventional way. On the spot, Whit invented this miracle: He allowed her parents to shuffle the cards, and then asked the blind child about the color of each card. She correctly divined the color of every card in the deck with complete accuracy. The mother and father were flabbergasted. What they didn't realize was that

Whit was coding the colors by tapping the girl's foot lightly: once for red and twice for black. When he left, he told the child not to ever tell her parents how she did it. She never did.

A short time later, Haydn received a package and a note from the blind child's mother. She thanked Whit for making her daughter the star, even for a few minutes, and told him that she felt empowered by being able to do something her parents couldn't do. The mother also sent him a deck of Braille cards so that he might develop more tricks to entertain audiences with visual impairments.

# Presto Prediction ON DVD

**MATERIALS: Jack of Hearts, Queen of Hearts, King of Hearts, the card box, a scrap of paper, and a permanent marker**    **LEVEL:** ♠ ♣ ♦ ♥

**K**nowing someone's choice before he or she makes it is impossible. It's a lot easier if you cheat! For this trick, you'll use an old magicians' principle called "multiple outs." That is, there are three different endings for the trick, depending on which of the three cards is chosen. Since you will never outline for your participants exactly how the trick will end, the spectators will assume the ending they experience is the only possible outcome.

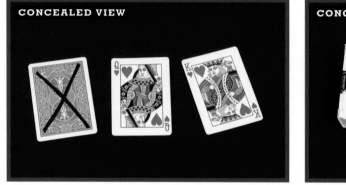

**1.** On the back of the Jack, draw a large "X" with a permanent marker.

**2.** On one surface of the card box, write "I knew you would choose the Queen."

**3.** Write on a piece of scrap paper "I knew you would choose the King." Then fold the piece of paper.

**4.** To prepare for performance, tuck the prediction inside the card box and place the three cards faceup on top. Then place the box on the table, writing side down. Now go recruit an audience.

**5.** Address your participant: "Life is about choices. The great aspect of making a decision is that only *you* can make a choice for yourself. But I'm going to prove to you that I already know a choice you will make— and you don't even know it yet." She will be skeptical.

**6.** Explain that this trick involves just three cards: The Jack, Queen, and King of Hearts. Present the box, taking care to keep the writing out of view. Remove the three cards faceup so as not to expose the X on the back of the Jack. Deal them faceup in a row.

**7.** "I would like you to choose one of the cards. But don't make it an obvious choice." If the participant is female, for instance, you might point out that she may want to avoid the Queen of Hearts because it would be too obvious, or she may indeed choose the Queen of Hearts because it *is* so obvious, rendering it improbable and thus unlikely to be predicted. Just play games with your participant, talking in circles, until she settles on a card.

**8.** Hand your participant the card box by gripping it from the sides, and ask her to place the card box on top of the card she has chosen, revealing it for the first time. She will receive the box, gripping it in the same manner that you hold it (which will minimize the chance of prematurely exposing the writing on the box's underside).

*Continued* ☞

**9.** The ending depends on which card is chosen—the principle of multiple "outs."

**a.** If she places the box on the Jack, turn over the King and Queen to display nothing written on the backs of the cards. Not impressive . . . yet. Now turn over the Jack of Hearts, revealing an indelible X across its back—an undeniably clear prediction of the participant's choice.

**b.** If she places the box on the Queen, ask her to turn the card box over and read the message intended for her. Another impressive ending.

**c.** If she places the box on the King, open the box and hand her the written prediction. She will read it and wonder how you could have known in advance. (You must remove the prediction from the box yourself and then display the box as empty. If you instruct her to do this, she could possibly discover the other out on the underside of the card box and realize the experiment is fraudulent.)

# HOFZINSER CARD

"Playing cards are the poetry of magic," magician Johann Hofzinser (1806–1875) once said. Hofzinser was the brain behind a fascinating gaffed card that had been all but forgotten until recently.

You already know that a playing card is comprised of three layers (see page 43). Hofzinser altered the middle layer of a card. When this card was placed in front of a candle, backside out, the candle would eliminate the pips on the innermost card. But when the card was turned around (and moved away from the candle), it would be seen to change to another card.

Lit from behind while spotlighting only a corner from the front allows you to see the card, and at the same time see through it.

# Friction Four

**MATERIALS: A new deck of playing cards**    **LEVEL:** ♠ ♣ ♦ ♡

**T**his instant four-card revelation is a cinch to execute with a crisp new deck. The location of all four Aces happens so fast that they seem to appear at your fingertips in a blur. Just preset the cards (Step 1) and then step right up to the card table.

**1.** Separate the four Aces from the deck and place two on top of the deck and two on the bottom.

**2.** Grip the deck facedown with the right thumb on top and the right finger pads below. The thumb should touch only the uppermost Ace and the finger pads only the lowermost Ace.

**3.** Cock the right wrist to the right and then jerk it sharply to the left, squeezing the top and bottom cards toward each other as you toss the rest of the deck into the awaiting left hand—never letting go with the right hand. In miming the tossing action, you actually release 50 cards into the left hand.

**4.** All the cards except the top and bottom Ace should have been propelled into the left hand. The upper and lower Ace remain in the right hand. Close your left fingers around the 50 cards using the same grip described in Step 2 with the left thumb above and left finger pads below.

**5.** In a continuous action, and again squeezing the top and bottom cards (the two remaining Aces) toward each other, toss the cards from your left hand back toward the right so they land across your working surface. *Hint:* While you had to toss the deck with some force to propel it into the other hand in Step 3, don't overdo it when tossing it to the table—the deck should land at least partially squared.

**6.** The second two Aces remain in the left hand after the tossing action.

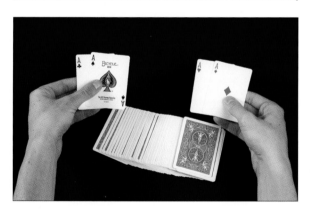

**7.** At the trick's conclusion, you're left with a pair of cards in each hand. Flip them over in your fingertips to dramatically reveal the four Aces.

## A CANCELED DECK

Casinos are the largest buyers and users of playing cards, and regulations allow a pack to be used for only about 8 hours before being exchanged for another. These rigid regulations help curb card tampering. So what happens to all the used decks? Every pack used on a casino table is "canceled" before it is resold. In the photo below, the pack has been canceled by drilling a hole through its center.

# Christmas Card

**MATERIALS: A deck of playing cards, rolls of green or red ribbon, a hole-punch, and a holiday tree!** **LEVEL:** ♠ ♣ ♦ ♥

T insel and candy cane decor is all played out. I suggest a new theme for the holidays: Vegas. "Deck" the halls (and the greenery) with all 52 cards for an economical, badass Christmas tree. The best part? This tree does tricks. So while this next trick does involve some serious commitment from the whole family, the payoff will be brilliant, especially when you can do it again, and again, and again.

**CONCEALED VIEW**

**1.** Punch a hole near the end of each card in a deck and thread red or green ribbons through each. Tie the ends in an overhand knot and trim the tree with your new ornaments!

**2.** Recruit a secret partner. A wife, husband, brother, sister—anyone will do. Together, you agree on a key card in advance, a predetermined card you will both remember. Suppose it's the Five of Spades.

**3.** At some appropriate moment, you invite everyone to gather around. "I realize our tree is decorated in an unorthodox manner this year," you say, "but as many of you know, I've developed a fascination with these ornaments. Believe it or not, this tree, with all 52 cards hanging from it, can do a trick." You call on a guest or family member to be your participant; let's say, Nate. "Nate, in a moment I'm going to leave the room. When I do, please walk over to the tree and pick any card."

**4.** After you've left the room, your participant selects a card by pointing to it (he shouldn't say it aloud or you might hear), let's say the King of Hearts. Then, you will have instructed him to take the selected card ornament, show it around, and replace it anywhere on the tree.

**5.** But you may notice that something on the tree has changed, so to make the conditions even fairer, everyone helps "shuffle" the tree. This means everyone will grab a card ornament or two, and move them to a different branch. This is when your partner does the dirty work. She will have noted the selected card (the King of Hearts), and retrieves the Five of Spades during the shuffling phase.

**6.** She hangs it directly to the right of the chosen card, in this case, the King of Hearts.

**7.** When you reenter the room, scan the tree until you find the key card (the Five of Spades). The card to the left is the participant's selection. You instantly determine the selected card ornament.

A card cascade is more for show than function, but there are very practical shuffles that are just as elegant.

# Chapter 3

# Shuffle Bored

**Trust your friends, but always cut the cards.**

—Anonymous

Sleight of hand has been my passion since I was eight years old: I can shuffle the hell out of a deck of cards. Over the years, I've had countless friends, audience members, and strangers—all embarrassed—ask me to teach them how to shuffle. But like all things in life, there isn't just one answer. There are myriad ways to mix up a pile of playing cards, and you're about to get a comprehensive tutorial.

In recent years, expert card handlers have elevated this simple task to an intricate art form. And beware the magician's shuffle: There's a good chance the shuffle isn't really mixing the cards (this is called a false shuffle). Casino shuffles, fancy flourishes, false cuts—it's all here. Even if you think you're a master mixer, much of what you're about to read will be new to you.

# Hindu Shuffle  ON DVD

**MATERIALS: A deck of playing cards**　　LEVEL: ♠ ♣ ◆ ♥

**M**agicians call this unusual way of mixing cards the Hindu shuffle, but it is by no means exclusive. When I was on tour in Asia doing magic shows, I found this way of mixing the standard. I guarantee none of your poker buddies mixes cards like this—you'll be the life of the party.

**1.** Begin by holding the deck at the sides, facedown between your right thumb and finger pads. As shown, the finger pads contact the deck at the inner edge, which allows the left fingers to access the front of the deck more easily.

**2.** Move your left hand underneath the deck, approaching it palm up.

**3.** Wrap the left fingers around the pack, pinching the top edges of the deck at the sides with the pads of your thumb and second finger.

**4.** Using these two fingers as pincers, grasp a small packet of cards (8 to 10 cards) and break them from the rest of the deck by lifting up slightly with the left hand.

**5.** Slide the left hand forward, away from your body, until the packet of cards in the left hand clears the rest of the deck.

**6.** Release the left second finger and thumb's grip on the packet, allowing it to fall into a rest position on the left palm.

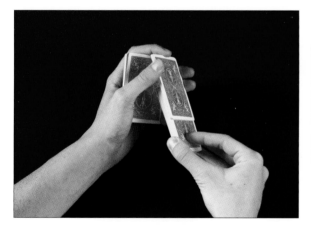

**7.** In a continuing action, approach the deck with the left hand, again from beneath, but this time with the addition of holding a packet. Don't let this packet of cards distract you; it doesn't affect the mechanics of the shuffle. Repeat the actions in Steps 2–4, taking another small packet between the pads of the second finger and thumb. The growing packet that rests on the left palm will not interfere with the move.

**8.** Again, slide the left hand forward and release the packet held between the left middle finger and thumb . . .

*Continued* 👉

**9.** . . . allowing it to pile on top of the first packet.

**10.** Continue shuffling in this manner until the entire deck has been transferred to the left hand. Then repeat. Concentrate on speed and neatness; it's important to take the packets *cleanly* into the left hand or the shuffle will look inelegant.

## THE POWER OF THE FORCE

Magicians sometimes use the Hindu shuffle you just learned for more devious practices: forcing a card. The same mechanics can be used to force a predetermined card on an unsuspecting spectator. She will believe her choice is random, but you will secretly know the identity of her card.

It's easy to learn. You must first secretly ascertain the identity of the bottom card of the deck; this will be the card you force. Then execute the Hindu shuffle as described, taking small packets of cards into your left hand. Ask a spectator to call "stop" any time she wishes. When stopped, separate your hands and raise the packet in your right hand, holding the face of the bottom card toward the spectator. Even though the bottom card doesn't change during the Hindu shuffle, the illusion of stopping randomly on this card is quite convincing.

How do you use this force? There are lots of ways, but here is an excellent one. After the force, bury the card and put away the deck. Say, *"We won't even use the deck. Just stare into my eyes and think of the name of your card . . ."* Now cock an eyebrow, take a deep breath, and announce the name of your force card.

# Tabled Riffle Shuffle

**MATERIALS: A deck of playing cards, a soft table surface**      **LEVEL:** ♠ ♣ ◆ ♥

**One of the most important differences between man and other species
is the opposable thumb, which allows man to both overhand and riffle shuffle.**

—STEVE BEAM, *Semi-Automatic Card Tricks, Volume 2*

**D**id you ever wonder why cards are always mixed with riffle shuffles in Las
Vegas? Nevada state regulations. For the protection of both the players and
the casinos, the cards are given tidy, tabled riffle shuffles. The tabled riffle shuffle's
actions are compact and precise, rendering it difficult to catch a glimpse or
secretly note the value of a card during a shuffle. With a casual overhand shuffle
or a mix in the hands, the bottom card in the deck is usually exposed to at least
one other player. Shuffles that involve a large riffling action risk exposing cards
near the top as they are riffled off the thumb. The riffle shuffle makes it difficult
for the peeled eyes of poker players and even the occasional crooked dealer. A soft
working surface is essential for this shuffle. Although you don't need casino-green
felt, it definitely adds atmosphere.

**1.** Begin with the deck facedown on the table, oriented sideways, as shown, and just left of your body's center point.

**2.** With the right thumb and fingers, cut approximately half the deck to the right. Place the cut-off packet ½ inch from the lower half, so that only a minimal amount of movement is necessary to weave the cards.

*Continued* ☞

**3.** Both hands will mirror each other from this point. Place your thumbs on the sides of the packets closest to you, just shy of the packets' centers.

**4.** The first fingers rest, curled, on top of the packets while the second and ring fingers brace the packets at the opposite sides. The little finger of each hand keeps the outer end of each packet squared.

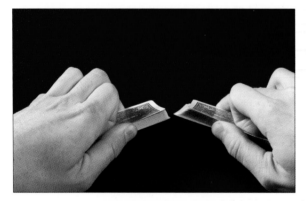

**5.** Lift the thumbs slightly, raising the inner corners of each packet. After both corners have been raised, both hands move (each as a unit) toward each other so that the cards' corners overlap.

**6.** Riffle cards slowly and simultaneously off each thumb, allowing the cards to weave at *only* the inner corner. *Hint:* Think soft and gentle; very little pressure is required to weave playing cards.

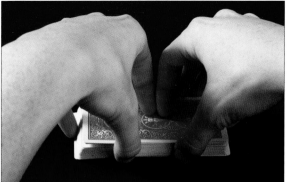

**7.** After all the cards have been riffled off the thumbs, straighten the little finger of each hand.

**8.** Move your hands together to square the cards, keeping each packet square against the flexed little fingers. The flexed little fingers brace the packets from the ends and help the cards slide together. Now you're ready to shuffle cards in Vegas.

## A FLUID RIFFLE

If you're having trouble doing the riffle shuffle fluidly, your grip is still too firm. Martin A. Nash, a close-up card magician known as the "Charming Cheat," gave a demonstration to emphasize the importance of gentle shuffling. He would open a brand-new deck of cards and ruin it in three casual shuffles. They aren't obnoxious shuffles; they are just firm, tense riffle shuffles. He purposely applied too much thumb pressure and held the cards too firmly as he riffled, causing the corners to bend and bow. After just three shuffles like this, the pack is worthless to a card handler. A gentle shuffle will save you aggravation and money.

# In-the-Hands Riffle Shuffle

**MATERIALS: A deck of playing cards**     LEVEL: ♠♣♦ ♥

**P**laying cards are addictive, and if I've done my job, you'll be toting them around with you everywhere (you know you're dedicated when there are spare packs in the glove box and bathroom). But in many of the places where you'll have cards, you'll be lacking a surface to put them on. This shuffle, also called a Dovetail Shuffle, is one I use all the time because it involves no table. If you're ever playing Spades in an airport or practicing your One-Handed Fans in a waiting room, this is your weapon of choice.

**1.** Grip the deck from above with the right hand. Curl the first finger on top of the deck so that the first and second knuckles rest on the top card.

**2.** Rotate the right hand so the thumb is uppermost. The left finger pads should be positioned on the face of the deck.

**3.** Riffle approximately half the cards off the right thumb onto the awaiting left fingers. Insert the left thumb into the break between the packets and grip the lower packet between the left thumb and fingers.

**4.** You can now separate the hands as each hand grips half the pack independently.

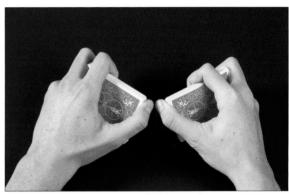

**5.** The right hand's grip on its packet is already correct, so no adjustments are necessary. Regrip the left packet, however, with the left thumb at one end and the fingers at the other. The grip and action of both hands should mirror each other.

**6.** You'll note that the packets are in a deep grip in each hand. That is, the outer end of each packet is aligned with the base of the fingers. Wrap the first fingers around their respective packets, allowing the pad of each first finger to contact the face card of each packet. The positioning of the first finger helps brace the packets from beneath (in lieu of a table).

*Continued* 👉

**7.** To execute the shuffle, riffle the cards in each packet off the thumbs, allowing them to weave together. Notice that in this shuffle, unlike the riffle shuffle, the entire ends of the packets overlap.

**8.** Use your fingers to gently push the card packets flush. It can and should be repeated, ad nauseum. Look, Ma, no table!

## CARD QUIZ

**Have playing cards saved lives?**

**Yes!** In 1943, the U.S. Playing Card Company began a secret project with the U.S. government. It printed small maps (scale: 1:100,000) indicating escape routes on the inside layer of playing cards. These cards were shipped to German POW camps as medical parcels or "donations." American prisoners could secretly soak these cards until the glue dissolved and the layers of the cards could be peeled apart. Reassembled as a full map, the cards would show suggested exit routes—which were used by prisoners in several successful escapes.

Today, the U.S. Playing Card edition is exceedingly rare.

# Overhand Shuffle

ON DVD

**MATERIALS: A deck of playing cards**     **LEVEL:** ♠ ♣ ♦ ♥

**N**o shuffling lesson would be complete without a tutorial on the venerable overhand shuffle; it's a rite of passage in most private games. But this shuffle is easily corruptible, so be mindful of its pitfalls (see sidebar, page 82). It should be noted that the overhand shuffle isn't thorough; it merely displaces large groups of cards, which is only one step above a solitary "cut." When money is on the line, do like the casino dealers and use more than one method of shuffling.

**1.** Grip the facedown deck from the bottom in your right hand, fingers at the outer end and thumb at the inner end. Angle your hand so the pack is at a 45-degree angle to the ground.

**2.** Move your left fingers under the pack as you rest the left thumb on top of the uppermost card.

*Continued* 👉

**3.** With your right finger and thumb pads, ease your grip on the uppermost 10 or so cards as the left thumb applies pressure on top of the deck. Allow this upper packet of cards to fall into the cradle of the awaiting left fingers.

**4.** Immediately repeat this action, sliding a small number of cards from the top of the right-hand packet and allowing them to fall onto the left-hand packet.

## ON DEFENSE

This book earns you a master's degree in shuffling, but invariably some guy will use the overhand shuffle in a game you're involved in (not everyone has the benefit of a higher shuffling education). You'll need to watch for two things when others use this shuffle. First, if the deck isn't held at a 45-degree angle, the bottom card will be exposed. Knowing the bottom card is an unfair advantage. Second, by taking only one card off the top at the beginning of the shuffle, this card will go immediately to the bottom (where an able cheat will deal it to himself or an accomplice using a bottom deal). And finally, while it may sound obvious, doing a faceup overhand shuffle should set off alarm bells in your head. Any capable cheat watching will likely know the identity and order of the top few cards, which is enough information to take the rest of the players for an expensive ride.

**5.** Repeat this action until you have transferred all of the cards from the right hand into the left.

# Faro Shuffle

ON DVD

**MATERIALS: A deck of playing cards**   LEVEL: ♠ ♣ ♦ ♥

Y ou're about to learn the most precise shuffle in the world. Several books have been written about the Perfect Faro Shuffle, the mathematics involved, and tricks that utilize it. You will perfectly weave two packets together. That is, the cards will alternate evenly between the packets. When you're proficient, it takes less than two seconds to weave all 52 cards—it takes considerably longer to master this skill.

**1.** Hold the deck facedown between the left thumb and finger pads, gripped on the sides toward the upper end of the pack. Curl the left first finger pad around the upper end of the deck. Move your right hand toward the left and grip the cards in much the same way: Situate the right thumb below the left thumb and place the right finger pads on the deck just below the left finger pads.

**2.** With your right thumb, riffle approximately halfway into the deck.

**3.** Break the deck at this point, taking the upper portion into your right hand.

**4.** Move the outer end of the right hand's half below the left hand's packet, and butt the ends together.

*Continued* 👉

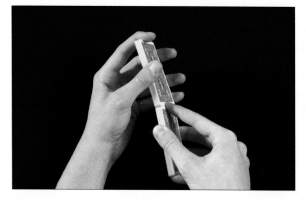

**5.** To keep both card packets square, extend the right first finger to the juncture between the packets and apply pressure.

**6.** To carry out the shuffle, push the packets together, applying more pressure to the inner side where the packets meet. Slide the upper, left-hand packet toward your body slightly, scraping it against the lower packet. These actions cause the first few inner cards to weave between each other.

**7.** When this happens, simply increase the pressure *slightly*. Like a zipper, the rest of the deck should follow suit. It can be tricky to start, but once the process begins, the cards weave seamlessly. The mechanics of starting the shuffle will vary depending on the condition of your cards, the humidity, and luck. Experiment with tiny movements of the left and right hand and different degrees of pressure to find what works best in each situation.

**8.** Assess: You may notice small imperfections in the shuffle (marked above), where two cards from the same packet remained together. With practice, you can get a perfect weave without these flaws. You may also notice a large block of cards on the top or bottom of a particular packet. This just means you didn't cut exactly 26 cards in each packet.

*Variations:* Most of you can live a fulfilled life without ever attempting a perfect faro shuffle. A normal faro is a thorough, silent way of mixing cards. However, if you do decide to learn perfect faro shuffles, here are three challenges.

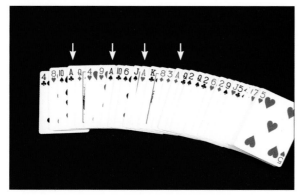

- **Stacking Four Aces:** Place four Aces on top of the pack and give it two in-faro shuffles ("in" means that the original top card, in this case an Ace, becomes the second card from the top after the shuffle). After the second in-faro, the Aces will be stacked for a four-handed game of poker so that each one falls to you, the dealer.

- **Perfect Giant Fan:** Now that you know the faro shuffle, revisit the Giant Fan (page 19). You will be able to do it much faster, and it looks markedly better with this extra bit of panache.

## FOLLOWING THE SHUFFLE

While it may sound difficult, magicians often rely on a perfect faro shuffle (see page 86). That is, we learn to split the deck at exactly the halfway point (26 cards in each packet) and then weave the cards perfectly. When done with this kind of precision, there's a world of possibilities. If you know a particular card's location, you can calculate its new location after the shuffle (for the curious, it's the card's current position multiplied by two, minus one . . . not that you asked).

If you do eight perfect faros in a row, you'll return the deck to the order it started in. Just make sure you do eight perfect "out" faro shuffles, which means at each shuffle's completion, the top and bottom cards remain the same.

# ONE-HANDED FARO SHUFFLE

**Playing cards have the ability to cloud men's minds, or to dominate them.**

—RICKY JAY, *in* Playing Cards *by Donald Sultan*

**F**ewer than a hundred people worldwide can execute a perfect, one-handed shuffle. It involves splitting the cards at exactly 26 and 26, aligning the edges, and then lightly pressing the edges together so that every card alternates. Perfect shuffles, with one or two hands, have fascinating mathematical potential. Eight perfect out-Faro shuffles restores the deck to its starting order. If four Aces are placed on top of the deck, after two perfect shuffles, the Aces will be positioned every fourth card, stacked for a four-handed game. How does the old saying go? Trust your friends, but always cut the cards.

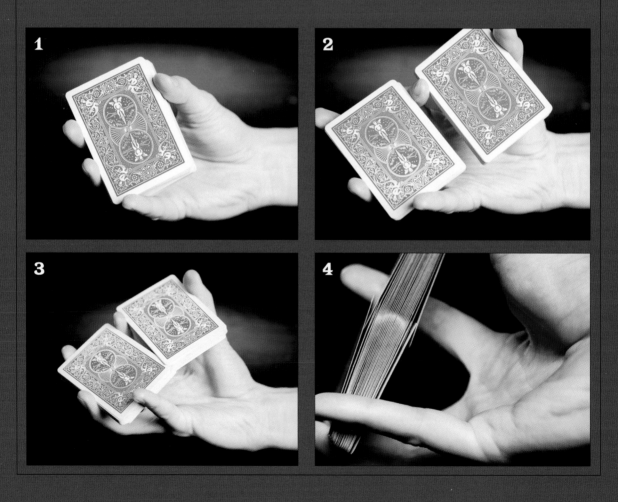

# The Bridge

ON DVD

**MATERIALS: A deck of playing cards** LEVEL: ♠ ♣ ♦ ♡

**W**hether you use a faro or a riffle shuffle, a bridge is a classy way to assemble the cards. After the cards have been woven but before they have been squared, try this classy flourish. And for those who can already perform a bridge, skip to the double bridge to learn something you've never seen.

**1.** For the classic card bridge, begin in a position where the ends of the deck have been woven. A faro shuffle (page 83) works ideally here because the weave is so thorough. You can also start an in-the-hands shuffle (page 78). Make sure the cards overlap about 1 inch.

**2.** Hold this extended "telescoped" pack horizontally, facedown between your hands, with the fingers supporting it from beneath and the thumbs resting on top. Apply pressure between the thumb and fingers of each hand to keep the cards in position.

**3.** With the deck in this clamped position, roll your wrists away from each other, causing the telescoped deck to bow. The finger pads continue to apply pressure below the bowed deck.

**4.** Make sure that the cards don't prematurely "spring" together during the bowing action, and position the thumbs at the apex of the bridge.

**5.** To execute the bridge, flatten the fingers beneath the telescoped pack.

**6.** The flattening of the fingers allows the cards from each packet to spring toward each other. With the thumb pads, push on the top of the deck to keep cards from flying out of your hands. This flourish can't be done slowly.

## THE JOKER

The evolution of the Joker card is erroneously attributed to the fool card in a tarot deck. Actually, this iconic card first appeared in 1865 in the game of *euchre,* a popular game among German-American immigrants. In this game, the most powerful card is the Jack of the Trump suit, referred to as the "best bower." In 1865, American cardmaker Samuel Hart created a special best bower card to replace the Jack. This card was named after the game its bearer would win: the euchre card. And "euchre" in German is *jucker.* Although euchre's popularity was replaced by poker, the *jucker,* or Joker, remains.

# The Double Bridge

**MATERIALS: A deck of playing cards**    **LEVEL:** ♠ ♣ ♦ ♥

**B**ridging cards is standard fare at poker tables worldwide. But bridging cards twice separates the men from the boys.

**1.** The double bridge begins in the same position as the bridge (page 88), gripping the telescoped pack with both hands. But, for the double bridge, it's essential that you use a faro shuffle to mix the cards. Place the partially shuffled deck in your left hand, gripping the pack where both packets are interlaced about 1 inch.

**2.** Move your right hand above the telescoped pack. Place your right second finger pad at the outer right corner of the outer packet and your right thumb pad on the inner left corner of the inner packet.

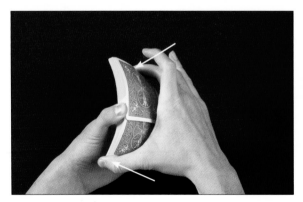

**3.** Apply pressure at these opposite corners of the telescoped pack. That is, bow the elongated deck upward as you apply diagonal pressure (see arrows).

**4.** Relax the pressure with your fingers, allowing the cards from each packet to spring toward each other. However, because the cards spring in slightly different directions, the packets remain segregated. That is, the outer packet gathers to the left of the inner packet.

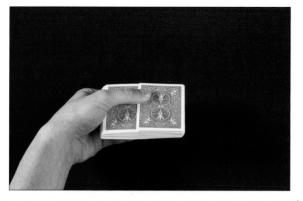

**5.** If you examine it closely, you'll see that although the packets are now square at the ends, they remain separated at the sides.

**6.** For the second bridge, regrip the deck from beneath with the palm-up left hand. The right hand supports the deck from above.

**7.** Bow the deck in a concave manner and then slowly release the pressure with your right index finger.

**8.** The cards will bridge again, this time from their sidestepped position.

**9.** At the conclusion, you'll be holding the deck squared in the left hand, ready to deal.

# CARD QUIZ

**Were the Kings originally *real* kings?**

**It depends upon whom you ask.** Playing card characters have had so many face-lifts and modifications that their origins are hard to trace. But in the 16th century, playing cards from Paris were modeled after legendary figures from the annals of history. The "Paris" Kings are representative of the four most influential civilizations of pre-medieval culture.

According to some accounts, all the court cards are modeled after distinguished figures in history. The English adapted the costume designs of the ancient Kings to the style of Henry VIII, which accounts for the 15th-century clothing still depicted on cards today. Here is just a sampling of the origins.

The Queen of Hearts may be originally modeled after the Hebrew heroine Judith (what luck—Mom always wanted me to spend time with a nice Jewish girl).

The King of Hearts may represent King Charlemagne of the Holy Roman Empire.

It is suggested that Julius Caesar is depicted on the King of Diamonds to represent the Roman army.

Enter Alexander the Great, King of Macedonia, the man some say is behind the King of Clubs.

The King of Spades may be modeled after King David (as in David and Goliath . . . minus the slingshot).

# *Really* Shuffle the Cards

**MATERIALS: A deck of playing cards, a table surface**     LEVEL: ♠ ♣ ♦ ♥

How many times do you have to shuffle a deck of cards to make the order truly random? If you answered seven, you may pass go and collect 200 Monopoly dollars. When real money is on the line, make sure the dealer shuffles *seven* times. Stanford University's Persi Diaconis made history in 1992 when he and associate David Bayer published results that showed how many riffle shuffles it takes to reach total randomization.

Using a riffle shuffle (as explained on page 75), at least seven shuffles are required before all order is lost (if you use a wimpy overhand shuffle, 2,500 times is necessary—you don't have that kind of time, so always use a riffle shuffle). Most casinos shuffle only two or three times, and Diaconis claims that an astute gambler can still discern certain properties of a deck's order after fewer than seven shuffles. And Diaconis would know—he's also a magician. A quick demonstration will easily prove how long order can be maintained during riffle shuffles.

**1.** Remove the 13 Spades from your deck of cards and order them from Ace to King, with the Ace on the face of the packet.

**2.** Place this packet of cards faceup on top of the facedown deck.

*Continued* 👉

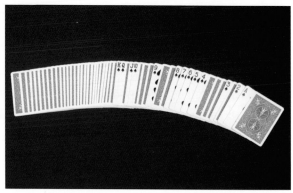

**3.** Cut approximately half the cards off the top of the deck and execute a riffle shuffle as you learned on page 75. Now ribbon spread the deck facedown on the table so that only the Spades appear faceup.

**4.** You'll see that despite the shuffle, all 13 Spades remain in order, with a few cards interwoven at various places. With this first shuffle, you've created two "chains" that are now interlaced. The chain we'll be following is the run of Spades.

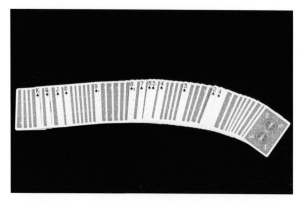

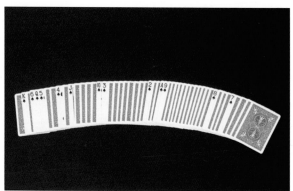

**5.** Square the pack and execute a second riffle shuffle. Cut the deck at about center, and ribbon spread the cards again to see that the 13 Spades are still in order, this time with a few more facedown cards between.

**6.** Square the cards and do a third riffle shuffle. Ribbon spread the cards again. At first glance, it appears the order has been destroyed. Actually, this isn't the case. With each shuffle, you're simply shortening your existing chains of cards and creating new chains.

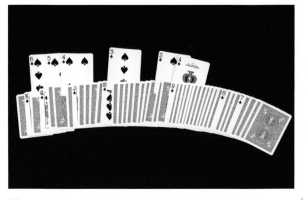

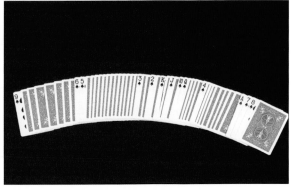

**7.** Find the Ace of Spades. Now find the Two of Spades, and then the Three. While there are facedown cards in between, and probably a few high Spade cards, you'll see that the *order* is still intact. (When you reach the end of the pack, simply start again at the other end.) The chain is still complete, but with each shuffle, the chain of Spades gets smaller and smaller until . . .

**8.** . . . the cards are truly mixed at lucky shuffle number seven.

## CRIME-FIGHTING CA[RDS]

In 2008, the South Caroli[na] [...] [correctio]ns implemented an offbeat method for solving crimes: They off[...] [...]s of unsolved crimes. The packs are regulation: 52 different cards [...] [B]ut on the face of each card is a murder victim, the circumstances [...] [t]o call for information (some cards even offer an anonymous tip line f[...] [detai]ls). One reads:

*The body of the vict[...] [...]d . . . the victim was [killed] in an unknown location and then place[...] [...]d, but with no shoes.*

A little gruesome, perh[aps...] [...] 10,000 decks have been sold in South Carolina, and the packs ha[ve...] [...]nd state agencies all over the country. Effective Playing Cards, the [...] [...]have been solved as a result of their efforts—including the case de[...]

# False Cut

ON DVD

**MATERIALS: A deck of playing cards, a table surface**    LEVEL: ♠ ♣ ♦ ♥

**W**ho would want to learn how *not* to mix cards? A cheater—that's who. In a game of cards, stacking the deck is only half the battle. Once the deck is stacked, the cheater must maintain his arrangement while giving the impression that the cards are being mixed. While we've already learned several ways of shuffling and cutting cards, this move merely simulates a cut. Actually, the order of the cards after the move is exactly the same as in the beginning. The key to this cut, popularized by magician Jay Ose, is all rhythm. As long as the cards are cut and then assembled in one slow, fluid sequence, it will look like a genuine triple cut. I'm certainly not suggesting you cheat at cards, but if you ever *do* go to the trouble of stacking a deck, I'd hate to see you accidentally shuffle away your winning hand. Basically, you'll be cutting the deck into three piles and then assembling those piles in the same order you cut them. Net effect: nothing.

**1.** Hold the deck in your left hand. Begin by cutting approximately a third of the deck with the right hand and placing it on the table, to your right.

**2.** Next, cut another third and place it to the left of the first packet.

**3.** Finally, take the remaining third of the deck into the right hand and place it on the table to the left of the other two packets.

**4.** With the right hand, scoop up the rightmost packet and plop it on top of the center packet.

**5.** Take the combined packet and slap it on top of the leftmost, bottom packet. Done in one fluid rhythm, it really looks like you've given the deck a triple cut.

## CARD QUIZ

**Shuffling cards is cool. But what is *un*shuffling?**

Unshuffling or "sorting" cards involves putting a shuffled pack back into order (Ace through King or King through Ace, segregated by suits). The current world record for sorting a pack of cards is 36.1 seconds, held by the Czech Republic's Zdeněk Bradáč.

Sorting cards is a growing industry. As of December 2000, the Warm Springs Correctional Center in Nevada introduced a card-sorting program for its inmates. Thirty inmates are selected to sort cancelled casino playing cards (see page 95) so they can be resold. We know that fast hands with a pack of cards can get you locked up, but apparently that's a skill worth having on the inside.

Jumping Jacks, a frog prince!, *page 100.*

# Chapter 4

# Cards and Crafts

**A pack of cards [is] a pile of 52 pieces of cardboard that can be bent, stacked, and stuck together in a seemingly endless array of variations.**

—JAY SANKEY, from *Art of Astonishment, Volume One*

You can't put a complete deck of cards through the mouth of a bottle. You can't hide valuables *in* a deck of cards. You can't send a playing card as mail. You can't tell the value of a card unless you look at its face. Or . . . can you? This chapter examines the many forms a deck of cards may take, introduces a new kind of "card cutting"—the kind you do with scissors and knives!—and redefines the postcard.

If mischief is your thing, we'll explore some amazing stunts you can do with these altered pasteboards. Just don't use these techniques taught here to cheat (or if you do, don't tell 'em where you learned about marked cards!).

# The Leap Frog

**MATERIALS: One playing card**          LEVEL: ♠ ♣ ◆ ♥

I n about a dozen folds, you will have a playing-card frog—and it even jumps. The advantages of an origami frog over an amphibious one are substantial: No feeding is required, it can be squeezed as hard as you like without making a mess, and you have a greatly diminished risk of getting warts. I don't think the Chinese had playing cards in mind when they were developing the art of paper folding, but magician Michael Close always has playing cards on his mind—and we have him to thank for adapting this origami classic to the pasteboard.

**1.** Place the card, let's say the Jack of Spades, faceup on the table.

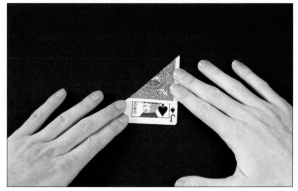

**2.** Fold the upper left corner diagonally so that the top edge lines up with the right side. Neatness counts.

**3.** Unfold and repeat with the upper right corner, folding it even with the left side.

**4.** Unfold again to reveal a creased X just past the card's center point.

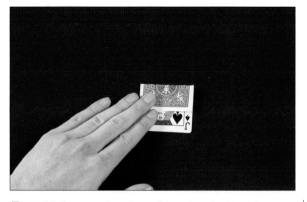

**5.** Fold the top edge down, bisecting the X with a straight fold and creasing through the X's center.

**6.** Unfold and then fold the card the opposite way (pattern side in), creasing well. Then unfold again.

**7.** With your fingers, apply light pressure on the sides of the card (on either side of the X), allowing it to collapse in on itself, creating a point at the X's center.

**8.** Flatten this unit along the creases. You've created a triangle with a rectangle beneath it.

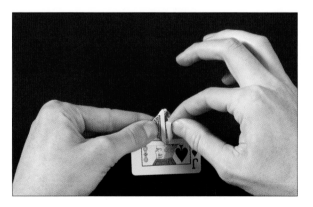

**9.** To make the frog's front legs, fold the top layer of the left and right points of the triangle to the triangle's top point, one at a time, as shown.

*Continued* ☞

**10.** Fold the left and right sides of the card so that they line up at the center.

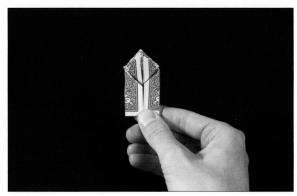

**11.** A diamond shape has formed at the top of the folded card.

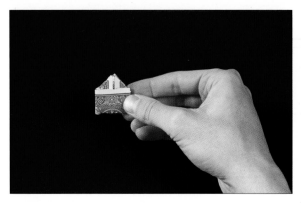

**12.** Fold the bottom of the card over the diamond, creasing at the base of the diamond.

**13.** Without releasing this bottom fold, fold the end back on itself halfway.

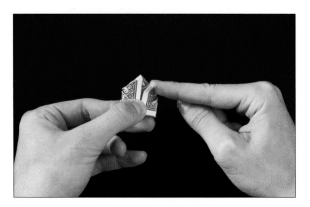

**14.** For some final touches, curl the front legs down slightly, being careful not to upset the frog. *Optional:* You may want to draw your new pet a couple of eyes or other identifying features.

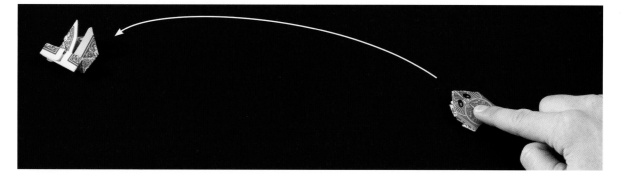

**15.** Now for the best part: Your frog does tricks! Press the pad of your first finger on his back and slide your finger backward, allowing him to pop into the air. The thickness of the playing card gives your frog some serious torque and air time.

## CARD QUIZ

**Why is a Jack called a Jack?**

**The three original court cards were King, Cavalier, and Knave** (to this day, Spanish, Italian, and German cards bear three male figures, no females). The French substituted the Queen for the Cavalier, but when manufacturers started using indices on playing cards, a problem arose. A capital Kg indicated King, or Qn for Queen, and Kn for Knave. The King and the Knave were often confused for each other, so the term Jack (a synonym for servant or knave) was implemented. Not many people know this, but most people don't know Jack.

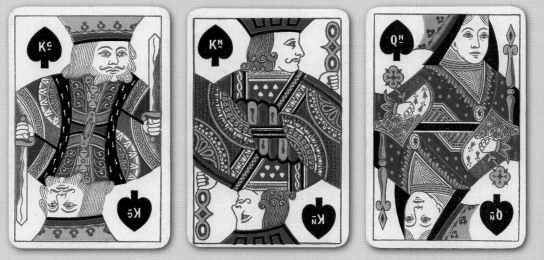

A King, a Knave, and a Queen from an English deck by Thomas De la Rue (1890).

# Cards in a Bottle

**MATERIALS: Empty flask-style bottle, a deck of cards, a pair of long tweezers**

**LEVEL:** ♠♣♦♥

A deck of cards doesn't do you much good when it's inside a bottle, but then neither does a toy ship. You're about to make a nice mantle ornament and a great conversation piece.

Besides a deck of cards, you'll need an empty bottle which you can pull from the recycling. Flask-style whiskey bottles work well for this because they're more flat than round and barely taller than a deck. When all the cards are in the bottle, the contents look snug because of the bottle's size.

**1.** Remove the label from the empty bottle by peeling, soaking, or scrubbing it off.

**2.** Take a playing card and roll it into a tube, just small enough to fit into the mouth of the bottle.

**3.** Pinch the top end of the card (where it overlaps itself) with the tweezers and gently push the card into the bottle.

**4.** Once the card clears the bottle's neck, release the card from the tweezers.

**5.** Use your tweezers to make small adjustments to the card to remove as much of the bend as possible.

**6.** Repeat. Repeat again. And again. And again. Remind yourself that the end result is worth the effort. Now just 47 more times.

**7.** When all 52 cards are in the bottle, you're done!

## CARD QUIZ

**What is the nutritional value of playing cards?**

**Unfortunately, cards are only food for the soul.** I would love to tell you that, in a bind, a human life could be sustained with cards, but there's only one kind of club sandwich worth eating—and it isn't the kind served on blackjack tables. Playing cards *are* pure fiber, but they are coated with chemicals that could be potentially harmful if ingested in large quantities.

# CARDS IN A BOTTLE

**I**'ve shown you how to get an entire deck inside a bottle, which is impressive. But some dedicated card lovers have taken this feat to new heights. The bottle pictured here, by Eric Leclerc, depicts a full pack of cards inside the box, with a ribbon tied around it.

How is it done? "I can't really say," says Leclerc, "but it took a long, long time."

# Playing Card Wallet

**MATERIALS: 9 cards, scissors, clear packing tape, and 2 laminate sheets (if you don't have access to laminate sheets, clear packing tape or access to a laminating machine will work)**    **LEVEL:** ♠ ♣ ♦ ♡

**M**ost people lose money with playing cards; this project will ensure you never do. This wallet will hold all your currency, and you can customize it to hold credit cards or other small items. When folded, it transforms into what looks like nothing more than a glossy stack of playing cards.

**1.** Place strips of tape, sticky side up, on your work surface. Overlap the strips ⅛ inch to ½ inch to create a sheet. Leaving about ½ inch between each card, place your nine cards on the sticky sheet in the configuration pictured above: Two rows of three cards, followed by three rows with only one card. Mix the cards faceup and facedown if you like, or use a row of Aces or Kings—get creative.

**2.** Place strips of tape, sticky side down, sealing the playing cards between the layers. As an alternative, you can also seal the cards into position using laminate sheets which allow for near-perfect accuracy in positioning the cards.

*Continued* ☞

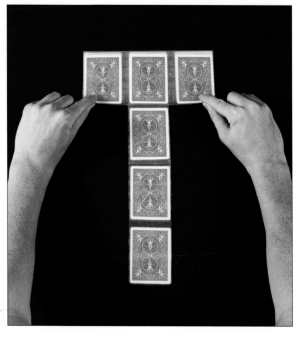

**3.** Cut along the edges of the card configuration, trimming off the extra tape. Take care not to trim between any of the cards; they must all remain connected.

**4.** To assemble the wallet, fold one row of three over the other.

**5.** Tape the sides of the foldover to create a pocket that is the body of the wallet.

**6.** Next, fold the body of the wallet behind the three-card column, to make the credit card slot. Two cards should protrude *below* the lower seam of the wallet.

**7.** Fold the lowermost card up, over the card it is attached to. Tape the sides of these two cards together to create a pocket with access at the top for credit cards or business cards. The pocket hangs beneath the wallet.

**8.** Fill 'er up! Load up your wallet pocket with business cards.

**9.** Then fold your wallet by first folding the hanging credit card pocket up. Then put the money in!

**10.** Now fold the sides together as you would any other trifold wallet.

Continued ☞

**11.** This wallet will fit conveniently in your front or rear pants pocket. The tape and laminate will conform to the contents of your wallet after a few hours, so the more you carry this playing card wallet, the better it will work.

*Variation:* Why stop at a wallet, when you can make a playing card purse? Ladies, forget Prada, Chanel, and Louis Vuitton, because Bicycle may just be the logo on the next "it" bag. Have on hand at least 32 cards, cloth tape or duct tape, scissors, an X-Acto knife, a cardboard sheet as large as you want the purse (to make a pattern), and access to a laminating machine. Make two side panels of cards with a row of cards connecting the two at the bottom of the bag (don't forget to cut out the handle). Finish it with a card bag tag. The specific bag design, card brand, and number of cards you use can be varied to match a particular outfit or embrace a certain style. For example, if you like red, you might consider using all Hearts or Diamonds. Or you might find a pack with an interesting back design; in this case you could orient all the backs outward. When you're done taping the seams together, place your wallet (page 107), keys, and essentials inside the purse—and be sure to leave room for a pack of cards.

# Post Card

**MATERIALS:** **At least one playing card with a lot of blank space (an Ace or Two), a small adhesive mailing label, and a postcard stamp**     LEVEL: ♠ ♣ ♦ ♥

T he United States Postal Service will deliver an addressed, stamped playing card about 80 percent of the time (based on my own experiments)—the odds aren't bad. But here are some ways of increasing your chances of success and some tricks to make the post really make an impression.

**1.** Start with a card that has lots of white space on the face, like an Ace or a Two. This way, you can write a small message to the recipient. I have a much higher success rate when I write some sort of message. Perhaps postal workers are more inclined to sort playing cards with the other mail if they feel you have something to say.

**2.** Write the address of the recipient on a small label and then stick that on the back of the card, along with a stamp. (It's incredibly hard to read anything written directly on a playing card's back design.) There isn't a lot of room for a return address on a playing card. (Plus, do you really want anyone to know *you* were the one who took the time to mail the Six of Spades?)

**3.** Take the card to the post office and hand it to an attendant (rather than just stuffing it in a mailbox). Sometimes the attendant mails it with a smile and sometimes he doesn't. If he tells you it's prohibited to send the playing card, tell him you've done it before, "at this very post office." That's what I did, and it worked.

*Continued* 👉

***Variations:*** If you have writer's block, here are a couple suggestions. Write "I knew you would pick this card" on the Four of Clubs and mail it to a friend. Before the card arrives in his mailbox, meet him for lunch and ask him to choose any card from your deck. Actually, you'll force him to choose the Four of Clubs (see the Ten-Twenty Force, page 48). Act like a bumbling magician and purposely find the wrong card. Eventually he'll get his selected card in the mail, postmarked a day or two *before* you did the trick. Next time, lunch will be on him.

Or, "Nothing says I love you like the Seven of Spades." Okay, that may be a stretch, but carrying a deck of cards is like having a Hallmark store in your pocket: 52 ways to show you care. The Queen (or King) of Hearts is an obvious, albeit contrived card to mail to a romantic partner: "To the Queen of my heart . . ." On Valentine's Day the Two of Hearts is a sappy but effective choice. Write on it, "The two of us belong together."

## WOW CARDS BY IAN ROWLAND

These hand-crafted impossibilities are designed and executed by British mentalist and friend, Ian Rowland. Nobody on the planet knows how he makes them, and a careful examination of each one reveals bends and overlaps that simply shouldn't be. When I look at these cards (which are a cherished gift), I experience all the emotions one feels watching a great card trick: Although it seems impossible, there must be a solution. But it's rather enjoyable to experience the impossible, and not know how it's done.

# Marking Cards

MATERIALS: **Complete deck of cards, a small knife**     LEVEL: ♠♣♦♡

**No one knows what is on the other side of a playing card.**

—José Hernández, *Martín Fierro*

**B**ut you will, in about 30 seconds. Here are three reasons to learn about marked cards:

1. To cheat people.
2. To protect yourself from being cheated.
3. For magic tricks.

"Readers," the gambler's term for marked cards, are not as common among cheats as one might suspect. An ambitious cheat will use judicious sleight of hand to improve his odds rather than gimmickry. Why? A marked deck is incriminating evidence, while a good bottom deal comes and goes as quickly as a lost wager.

Marking systems vary with every back design—and explaining how to mark a specific company or brand's back design would not make that company's executives happy. So, I'll offer you some general advice, teach you a fabulous magic trick (see reason no. 3), and then show you a preventative technique (see reason no. 2).

The particulars of marking a deck aren't critical; if people question the deck in use, then the cheater is being far too transparent with his methods. A good cheater will win only marginally more than other players, banking on small profit margins over long card sessions.

**1.** Choose a deck of cards with a busy back design and look for a portion that can be altered in several different ways. For instance, many back designs have flowers or petal designs. Or perhaps angels (shown). You can scratch away a different aspect of this design, depending on the card.

*Continued* ☞

**2.** An efficient way of marking a deck is called "scratching." Counterintuitively, rather than adding marks, *remove* small portions of the back design. With a small knife, gently scratch away the coloring on a card's back. For instance, if the back of the card features an angel design, you can scratch out the center of one or both of an angel's wings.

**3.** Since most cards have a two-way back design (which means if you rotate them 180 degrees, the design appears the same), you never know which way the card will be oriented—so the cards need to be marked twice, once on each end. Once you've got a marked deck, you have to practice reading it without concentrating intently. Subtlety is the key here. If you are drawing and discarding your cards without looking at their faces, other players may get suspicious.

## LUMINOUS READERS

**The cheater is generally the player one would least suspect.**

—LAWRENCE SCAIFE, *Spotlight on the Card Sharp*

Like something Q would devise for James Bond, luminous readers actually exist. These special glasses allow the wearer to see markings on cards that cannot otherwise be seen. The special dye used to mark the cards is invisible to the naked eye, but apparent when viewed through lenses that filter out the red color on the back of a deck. These gadgets are more interesting than practical, and there is little documented evidence of their use during real play.

***Variations:*** Marked decks often convey only certain information; it is not always necessary to encode a card's complete identity.

■ Sometimes just the four Aces are marked by scratching away the very corners of the cards (above). Since suits are less than critical in most games, all four Aces can usually be marked the same way. Similarly, many decks are just marked for "rich" (high) cards: Tens, Jacks, Queens, Kings, and Aces.

■ While some cards are marked by removing part of the design or inking, some can be marked by adding features. Cards that have a flock of birds as part of the design can be marked to have more birds.

■ Suits are marked in the same fashion as values. Search for a distinguishable part of a back design, perhaps an angel. Shown clockwise from top left, block out, say, the left wing for Clubs. Block out the right wing for Hearts, the head for Spades, and the torso for Diamonds.

# METICULOUSLY MARKED CARDS

This particular device, never before shown in print, is used to help the cheat systematically and more precisely mark cards. The playing card is aligned with measured grooves. A pen can be used to mark cards, or a blade can be used to scrape away ink (called the blockout technique; page 113).

So where does the cheat obtain his nefarious gizmos and gadgets? You can't exactly go to the cheating supply store, or can you? The K.C. Card Company was a thriving business originally located in Kansas City (they moved when the city pressured them out). The business began in the '30s and flourished for over thirty years, with buyers from every corner of the country. Some were curious, and others were professional cheats. The page depicted below shows an array of marked decks that K.C. Card Co. offered for sale. When K.C. Card Co. finally closed its doors, it boasted a mailing list of over 40,000 cheats—I mean customers.

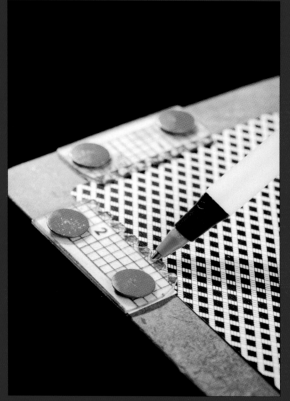

# Marked Miracle

**MATERIALS: A marked deck of playing cards (see page 113)**     LEVEL: ♠ ♣ ◇ ♥

**Y**ou'll need your marked deck for this incredible card trick (you know, the marked deck you made for "novelty" purposes only?). In this trick, you are not only able to locate a participant's chosen card—big deal—but then she, to her surprise, finds *your* chosen card.

**1.** Begin by handing a pack of cards to a participant and asking her to shuffle them.

**2.** Then ask the participant to cut the cards. Have her keep one half of the deck and give the other half to you.

**3.** Spread your packet facedown between your hands and invite her to take one card. As she takes the card from the pack, secretly note the card's identity from its markings. If you can't see markings on the card, you used the wrong deck.

*Continued* ☞

**4.** Remember the participant's card (let's say it's the Three of Hearts) and allow her to insert it back into your packet. At this point, since you already know her card, you (or she) can shuffle your card packet as much as desired.

**5.** Introduce the idea of reversing roles. "I'm going to try to find the card you selected—but I'm a magician, and that's my job."

**6.** "It would be far more impressive if you could do the same trick for me. Let's try." Ask the participant to fan her cards from hand to hand.

**7.** Take a card. Let's say it's the Two of Spades. Look at the card but don't remember it—easy enough. Take care that no other onlookers see your chosen card. Then insert the card back into your participant's packet and invite her to shuffle.

**8.** "There's a chosen card in each of our packets. I'll remove one card, the card I believe you chose. I'd like you to remove the one I picked." She may doubt her ability but encourage her to play along and guess which card you picked. Of course, you know which card she chose. Fan your pack of cards toward yourself and remove her card, keeping it facedown.

**9.** Ask your participant to hold your supposed card facedown, too. Then ask her for the name of her card. Turn over the card you hold to reveal a correct divination. Meanwhile, use the moment you turn her selection faceup to glimpse the identity of the card she removed for you—by reading the markings on its back.

**10.** Instruct your participant to ask you for the name of your card, despite her skepticism about getting it right. Tell her the name and then ask her to turn over the card she predicted . . . a perfect match. Advise her: "Use your powers only for good."

# ✑ CARD PUNCH ✑

You've heard of marked cards, and you should be wary of them when playing with strangers. But remember that marked cards aren't always visible. Cheats often employ cards marked tactilely. The device pictured below is a card punch, and it allows the cheat to put one or more bumps in a card's surface so he can feel the values of the cards as he deals. The bumps are smaller than Braille—no bigger than the head of a pin—and the pricks don't actually pierce the surface of the paper.

Instead, the bumps are raised only enough to be felt by a sensitive touch. Typically the cards are punched only so the dealer can differentiate high cards from low cards.

Cheats have even developed a way to punch cards during play, right under the noses of the other players. The cheat conceals a sharp point in a Band-Aid (below) and punches the high cards during the first few rounds of play. When it's his turn to deal, he can feel for the best cards in the pack, and deal them as he pleases.

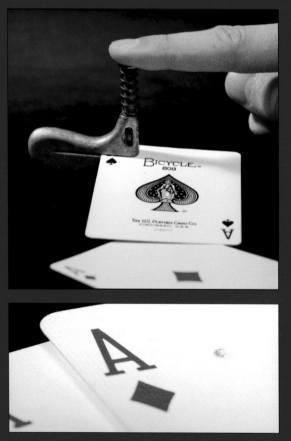

# Card Concealer

**MATERIALS: A deck of playing cards, the card box, and a craft knife**    LEVEL: ♠ ♣ ♦ ♥

I saw the strangest travel product in a catalog recently: It was a secret container to hide valuables. Cleverly disguised as a can of WD-40, the bottom of the can unscrews to reveal a secret compartment for jewelry, money, or valuables. Models were also available in cans of paint. I have to admit, these things look authentic. Now, the theory is sound, but the idea doesn't work. "Okay, things to pack: toothbrush, underwear, reading material, and a small can of forest-green paint." Who travels with industrial lubricant? I would think these objects would *arouse* suspicion in a suitcase rather than deter any would-be thieves.

That's when the idea hit me: A deck of cards would be a great place to hide some small valuables. Many people travel with a deck of cards: It's small, lightweight, and a useful way to pass travel time. Plus, it's appropriate to take with you in your carry-on luggage. It'll take you an hour to make, but if you travel even minimally, it's an hour well spent. Basically, you're hollowing out a deck of cards. You'll cut out a large portion of the center of each card, and when lined up, these prepared cards form a large hole.

**1.** To begin, place two cards aside. These will function as the top and bottom of this makeshift hiding place.

**2.** Take one of the remaining 50 cards, turn it facedown, and carefully cut out the center with a craft knife, leaving a ⅜-inch border, as shown. (Don't let the frame get too thin, or it will be flimsy.)

*Continued* ☞

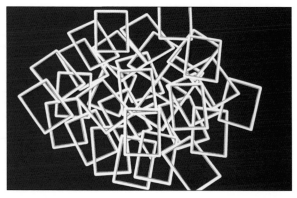

**3.** In order to cut the cards uniformly, look for a guide on the back of the card—the inside edge of a border or other repeated design—and continue to cut.

**4.** Repeat until the rest of the 49 cards have a window cut from the middle.

**5.** Stack the 50 prepared cards and place one of the two normal cards at the bottom of the prepared deck.

**6.** Insert your cuff links, keys, or other valuables into the recess.

**7.** Place the second normal card on top.

**8.** Slide the whole unit into the card box. Even if someone is snooping and opens the card box's flap, it still looks like the box holds a simple deck of cards.

# CARD SHAVING

The device below is used to trim off a fractional amount from a set of good cards (Aces or high cards). The amount shaved is so small that it is nearly impossible to detect visually. But when the shaved cards are placed in the deck, someone with a light touch can cut to them every time. The cheat may invite another player to cut the cards. Odds are favorable that even an unsuspecting player will unknowingly cut to a shaved card.

Trust your friends, but *always* cut the cards.

# Chapter 5

# Cheap Tricks

**A deck of cards is the perfect tool for deceit.**

—DAVID BRITLAND AND GAZZO, *Phantoms of the Card Table*

Seventeenth-century clergymen (not exactly my target audience) referred to playing cards as "The Devil's prayer book" or "The Devil's picture book," and outlawed them

because they could be—and were—used as tools for deception. My, things have changed. Cards in and of themselves are fairly innocent instruments—they're mere illustrations on cardboard, after all. It's what the card handler does with them that gives them the power to save lives, win fortunes, solve crimes (see page 95), or (gulp) draw blood. But rest assured, you can use every prank featured in this chapter with almost no risk of being burned at the stake.

# Fake Marked Cards

ON DVD

MATERIALS: **A deck of playing cards**  LEVEL: ♠ ♣ ♦ ♥

**B**eing caught using marked cards isn't funny unless you enjoy life without the use of opposable thumbs. But accusing someone else of using marked cards can be hilarious. Every poker game has one insufferable player—you know, the one who clouds up your basement with cigar smoke and eats all the salsa. Just remember, the bigger he is, the harder he falls. *Note:* I hate stating the obvious, but be sure to use someone else's deck for this. Proving that you can read the marks on *your* cards is counterproductive and, depending on your opponents, dangerous.

**1.** Between rounds, when it's your turn to shuffle, act as though you've been offended. "What's going on here? These cards are marked!" Spread through the cards, studying the backs carefully. Draw on your best acting abilities because, obviously, the cards aren't actually marked. Look at the person winning most frequently and accuse the poor sucker of marking the deck. He will squirm in his chair and turn redder than the King of Hearts.

**2.** Offer to explain. To prove the cards are marked, ask someone to shuffle the cards and then cut off a packet of about 10 cards.

**3.** Take the packet and spread through it facedown, shaking your head and feigning disappointment: "Really? Marked cards? I thought we were friends." Square the packet and hold it in your right hand by the ends, fingers above and thumb below.

**4.** Hold the packet with the faces toward the audience at chest height. Bow the cards (so they arc toward you) by squeezing the fingers and thumb toward each other.

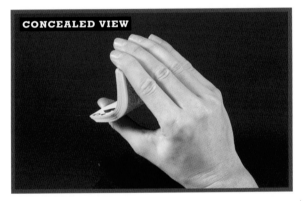

**5.** Interestingly, if the cards are held in this position at the right height, you should be able to clearly see the face card's index at the lower left corner. Remember this card—let's say it's the Five of Spades.

**6.** Using the left finger pads, slide the face card into the left hand. Hold the card normally in the left hand so you cannot possibly see the face. Now that you're in a position where you can't see its identity, stare intently at the card, as if reading the marks on its back. Shout out its name, which you already know (in this case, the Five of Spades).

*Continued* ☞

**7.** Before you peel the new face card from the right hand's packet with your left fingers, glimpse the identity of the new face card as you did in Step 5 by bending the cards as described above. For variation (shown), you can also glimpse the face card of the packet in your right hand under cover of a pointing gesture: Before dropping the card in your left hand, point to a spot on the back of it with your right first finger. Say, "I can see the mark right there," and point to any spot on the back of the card in the left hand. As you point, bend the right packet as explained and catch a glimpse of the next card.

**8.** Then slide the face card from the right hand into the left, stare at the back of the card for a few seconds, and then call out its value and suit. Repeat this stunt until either you run out of cards or the other players declare mob rule.

## DON'T GET CAUGHT

**Someone is cheating. I had three Aces in my lap and now they are gone!**

—U. F. GRANT

Getting caught cheating is no fun. Just ask Three Fingers Willie. Back when he was just Willie, he was one of the finest cheats on the 19th-century riverboats. But when he was caught with an oily marking putty on two fingers (called daub), the disgruntled players removed the putty for him—along with the fingers.

17th-century card cheats at work on their mark.

# Tearing a Deck in Half

**MATERIALS: A deck of playing cards, a small hacksaw**     LEVEL: ♠♣♦ ♥

I f you like to break stuff, this next one is for you. Not only will you have to prepare the deck in advance with a saw, but you'll also ruin the deck every time you do it—so stock up on cards and buy them in bulk. It's a shame this one likely won't become the runaway hit in this book (unless you're in possession of a truck full of card decks you're trying to unload), since it is a truly amazing stunt that has a huge impact on people.

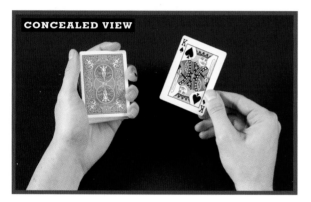

**1.** Tearing an entire deck of cards in half, at once, is impossible for most mortals . . . unless they start with the deck secretly torn. Remove one card from the deck for a moment and place it aside.

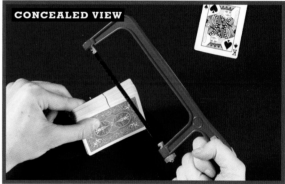

**2.** Now saw a small notch through one side of the rest of the deck, about ½ inch in from the edge.

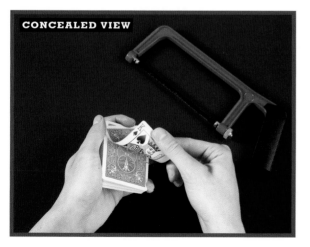

**3.** Place the card you set aside in Step 1 on top of the deck to cover the notch from view.

*Continued* ☞

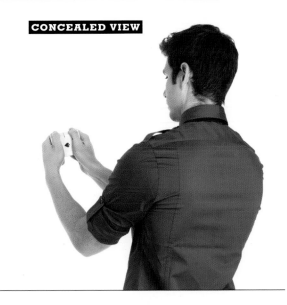

**CONCEALED VIEW**

**4.** Hold the cards in your hand, go to a place where there are lots of people, and act pissed. Really pissed.

**5.** After some preliminary cursing and kicking, shift your attention to the pack of cards. Grip the deck in both hands, thumbs on top and fingers beneath. The notch should rest on the upper side of the deck.

**6.** Move both hands in opposite directions, slowly tearing the deck in half. You won't have to mimic strain here, because you really *will* be straining to tear the deck; tearing even a small packet of cards is difficult.

**7.** Take the pieces, toss them into the air, and walk away. The reactions you'll get with this stunt make it worth ruining a deck. You have to try this to understand what I mean.

## DEAD MAN'S HAND

On August 2, 1876, Wild Bill Hickok entered Saloon No. 10 in Deadwood, Dakota Territory, his favorite poker haunt. His normal seat—looking out from a corner—was taken. He liked that seat because he was leery of an ambush from behind. But that night, he sat with his back to the door.

Jack McCall approached Hickok from behind that evening and shot him in the back of the head with a .45-caliber revolver, an act McCall said was revenge for his brother's death (he claimed Hickok had killed his brother, of which there is inconclusive evidence). Hickok had been losing that night, but when he died, he was holding a pair of Aces and a pair of Eights, all black, henceforth known as the Dead Man's Hand.

# SHINERS

**Fortunately, we know what cheats are up to. At least, we think we do.**

—DAVID BRITLAND AND GAZZO, *Phantoms of the Card Table*

Shiners (cheaters call them "glims" or "twinkles") are hidden mirrors that secretly reflect the identities of facedown cards to the dealer. Cheaters have hidden mirrors in virtually any object you might find at the card table: on or in a ring (below), a watch, glasses, the end of a cigarette, and even the inside of a pipe (below, right). And the technology is getting even sleeker. A shiner was recently uncovered within a playing card (right), secreted by a folding flap. Today, the most common form of a shiner is an upturned cell phone. At the right angle, in the right light, the screen gives off a perfect reflection of cards sailing from the dealer's hands, passing above the phone's screen.

Shiners render most marked decks obsolete because they can be used at any time with any deck. For the cheater, it's like playing with the cards faceup.

# Memorizing a Deck

*ON DVD*

**MATERIALS: A deck of playing cards**     **LEVEL:** ♠ ♣ ◆ ♥

To make your buddies think you memorized an entire deck of cards (which they can shuffle beforehand), you actually only need to remember one card and count from 1 to about 20.

**1.** Announce that you will memorize a deck of cards after another player has shuffled it. Hand out the deck to be shuffled. As she completes the mixing, secretly remember the bottom card of the deck. If the card isn't visible, take the deck back and look at the bottom card. Let's assume it's the Three of Clubs (magicians call this a "key" card).

**2.** Holding the deck of cards in your left hand, invite the participant to cut off a packet and instruct her to hold it in her hand.

## CARD QUIZ

**Can people *really* memorize a shuffled deck of cards?**

**Amazingly, yes!** On November 3, 1994, Tom Groves memorized a shuffled deck of cards in 42.01 seconds without a single error. But rumor has it that after the event, he couldn't remember where he parked. On November 26, 1993, Dominic O'Brien memorized 40 decks of cards (2,080 cards total) in a single sighting with only one mistake, setting the world record (for memorizing cards, not mistakes).

**3.** Now ask the participant to look at the card on top of the packet still in *your* hand—the card she cut to—and remember it.

**4.** After she commits the card to memory, ask her to place her selected card on top of the pile in her hands.

**5.** To apparently bury the card, plop the packet in your hand on top of her cards. The card appears buried somewhere in the deck, but it's actually right next to your key card on the bottom of the deck, in this case, the Three of Clubs.

**6.** Take the deck back and spread through the cards quickly with the faces toward you. Using your best acting skills, act as if you are memorizing every card as it goes by. In truth, you're spreading through the cards until you find the key card, the Three of Clubs. The card to its immediate right is the spectator's card, but you don't even have to remember it. Instead, just count every remaining card, starting with the selection, until you reach the end of the deck.

*Continued* ☞

**7.** Let's assume the selection is 16th from the top. Turn the deck facedown, hand it to your friend, or smack it facedown on the table and announce, "I just memorized the entire deck!"

**8.** Ask the participant which card she picked. Once she answers, pretend to concentrate intently, as if trying to recall the position of the selected card. After the appropriate period of head-scratching, tell everyone that the card just named is at the 16th position (or whatever number) from the top. Allow the participant to deal the cards one at a time. When she reaches 15, stop her for a moment.

**9.** "If I'm correct, the 15th card should be the Three of Clubs, and the next one should be yours." Here, as an added touch, you merely call out the name of your key card when you reach its position, just before the selection. By calling out this card at its position in addition to the selected card, the implication is that you really did memorize every card in the deck. Allow her to deal the last card and turn it faceup, "proving" that you memorized an entire deck of cards.

**10.** Now would be a good time to shuffle the cards before some jerk starts quizzing you on the order of the other cards.

# Getting Mental

**MATERIALS: A deck of playing cards, a friend, a table surface**      LEVEL: ♠♣♦ ♡

Reading a person's thoughts is impossible, but your friends will swear you have telepathic abilities after this stunt.

You will communicate the identity of the chosen card through a secret code known only to you and your accomplice. I've designed the code so that it is easy to remember and therefore easy to teach someone on the spot or at the bar—this "sixth sense" mystique stuff goes over great at parties.

Here's the scenario, as your spectators will see it. Your friend, the "receiver," will leave the room while a card is selected. Once the receiver is gone, you'll ask someone to think of a card. When the receiver returns, you'll look each other in the eyes with your fingers on your temples, apparently sending the thought of the card. After a brief mental struggle, the receiver can correctly name the chosen card.

**1.** Your friend (accomplice) leaves the room. You take the cards from the box and table the box at the center of your working surface. This will function as a visual guide to your friend.

**2.** A participant selects a card, say the King of Spades.

*Continued* ☞

**3.** Think of the table as the face of a clock and the box as the clock's center (no hands on this clock, of course). The value of the chosen card is coded by where you place the pack of cards in relation to the box.

**a.** If it's directly to the box's right, it's 3:00—and the chosen card is a Three.

**b.** Slightly higher, at the 2:00 position, and the selected card is a Two.

**c.** Below the box and slightly to the left is 7:00, which means the spectator chose a Seven.

**d.** Cards directly to the left of the card box indicate a Nine, and so on.

**e.** Jack is 11:00 since the Jack's worth is 11.

**f.** Queen is represented by the 12:00 position.

**4.** There is no hour equivalent for the King, which in this case, was the participant's selection. For a King, simply place the cards on top of the box.

**5.** This stunt can be repeated ad nauseum, but to throw off anyone watching for patterns, you can vary the distance of the pack from the box; that is, the cards are still placed in the correct time zones, but the appearance changes. *Example:* You may code a chosen Three by placing the pack an inch from the box and the next time you might code a Three by placing the deck two feet away from its box.

**6.** After the card has been chosen and you've noted the number or face and suit, shuffle the card back into the deck and table it in its proper place. Ask someone to retrieve your friend.

*Continued* ☞

**7.** A quick glance at the table will tell your friend the value (deck on box = King) of the chosen card, but the suit remains a mystery. The suit is coded with the first letter of the first word of the first sentence you say to her. There are four suits in a deck: Hearts, Clubs, Spades, and Diamonds, or H, C, S, and D. You'll invite the receiver to interpret your thoughts in one of four ways:

- Hearts: "Here, try this one" or "Have a go at this."

- Clubs: "Can you give this a try?" "Close your eyes and concentrate."

- Spades: "See if you can guess Jon's card" or "Stop right there. What card am I thinking of?"

- Diamonds: "Do you know what card Mary thought of?" or "Don't worry about everyone else, just concentrate on the card."

Since the chosen card's suit is Spades, your verbal cue must start with the letter S.

**8.** Psychology and acting are of equal importance here. Even though your friend will know the identity of the chosen card within seconds of entering the room, she must feign struggle before revealing the card. Your acting is important, too. Look her in the eye and squint—sending thoughts would be a draining process, right?

You can also enhance this scam verbally. Always try to reiterate that the cards are truly chosen at random by the participants. "See if you can guess the card Mike thought of." From your wording, it sounds as if your friend might even be intercepting Mike's thoughts—a feat more impressive than reading just one person's mind. "Come here. Angela thought of a card and she *swears* she didn't tell you. What card is she thinking of?"

**9.** By diverting all the attention to Angela, many viewers will forget you even saw the card, making it all the more amazing when your friend correctly identifies the randomly thought-of card: the King of Spades.

# STATIC STING

**F**ortunately for you, I did all the beta testing for the material in this book; I set 'em up, you knock 'em down. But apparently a lot of authors didn't test the following stunt before re-describing it in print. You'll exploit these people and those who have read the "outdated" version of this stunt. Just use some double-stick tape and do exactly what I did in the story that follows.

You see, the smooth linoid finish used on almost all playing cards is a technology that's less than 40 years old. Before that, cards felt more like cardboard. And if you look in old books on card games, a stunt of static electricity is often described whereby you hold a card, shuffle your feet across a stretch of carpet, and then stick a playing card to a nearby wall. Because of the static electricity built up through your body, the cards with the old finish would cling to walls for a short period of time.

News flash: This doesn't work anymore. Still, some people *swear* this works, despite never having actually performed it. And when one particularly hopeless soul started dragging his feet and pressing a card against a wall to prove me wrong, this gag was born.

I used to perform at a country-club function every year, doing tableside magic for the guests. A woman approached me and asked if I had ever seen how a card will stick to a wall with static electricity. She was so confident that I didn't have the heart to tell her that unless she was twice as old as she looked, she could never have done what she was saying she did. I always carry double-stick tape with me in case one of my props needs a last-minute fix. When she turned away, frantically trying to prove that a card can stick to a wall with static electricity, I applied a piece of double-stick tape to the back of the card. "Let me try that." I did the static walk thing, reached as high as I could, and adhered the card out of her reach. By this time a crowd was forming. "I got it!" I asserted.

This only frustrated the woman more, because no matter how hard and fast she shuffled her feet, the card fluttered to the floor, static-less. I immediately began passing out cards to all the people watching, and within minutes I had 15 middle-aged men and women, all dressed in formal suits and cocktail dresses, dragging their feet across the carpet, desperately trying to replicate the stunt I had just performed. One lady finally asked me how long the card would typically stay stuck to the wall. "Until I peel the tape away," I answered.

I didn't get hired the following year.

# Back Breaker

**MATERIALS: A deck of playing cards**     LEVEL: ♠ ♣ ♦ ♥

**Y**ou take a deck of cards in your right hand and hold it behind the back of your neck, clearly out of your range of vision. You dramatically place your left hand behind your back, at waist level. The spectators watch skeptically. You then spring the cards from your right hand down the length of your back and catch them in the left hand. Jaws drop to the floor—but wait, you're not done. For the grand finale, you shoot the cards in your left hand *back up* into your awaiting right fingers.

I can't teach you this because it's impossible. But, I *can* teach you a simulation so that your spectators will believe you actually did it. Best of all, it's easy.

CONCEALED VIEW

**1.** Start by cascading cards (page 33) from one hand to the other in front of you. Then announce, "That's nothing. Check *this* out."

**2.** Your audience should be in front of you. Also make sure there is nobody to your immediate left and right. Hold the deck at the ends in your right hand. Position the deck behind your neck, out of sight. Move your left hand behind your back at waist level.

**3.** It is important that you explain exactly what you're attempting to do. Since the whole stunt is implied and never actually seen, it's important you paint a vivid image. "I'm going to spring these cards from my right hand to my left—but behind my back!"

CONCEALED VIEW

CONCEALED VIEW

**4.** Like shooting a free throw, this stunt is all in the knees. Two things will happen simultaneously. You will riffle your right thumb along the top left corner of the pack and you will bend slightly at the knees, moving your whole upper body down a few inches, as if catching the cards. Strain your face a little, roll your eyes around, grimace—remember, this is supposed to be difficult.

**5.** Pause a few beats. "Now for the hard part. I'll shoot them back up." So saying, riffle the cards again with your right thumb as you did in Step 4, this time straightening your body as you do.

**6.** Immediately after riffling, move your right hand back over your head and into view as you comment, "Oh, look, I caught them all this time." As if you ever miss . . .

The Aleister Crowley tarot card deck, one of the most beautiful examples of this fortune-telling tool, *page 154.*

# Chapter 6

# Wild Cards

**I stayed up one night playing poker with tarot cards.**
**I got a full house and four people died.**

—STEVEN WRIGHT

**I**n a game, wild cards are cards that can be used for anything—to complete a royal flush or a straight, or to make a pair a three-of-a-kind. In this chapter you'll make your

whole deck into wild cards, using them in unexpected, new ways to build biceps, repel adversaries, keep time, and tell fortunes. Far beyond the shuffled bridges in Chapter 3, get ready to sign yourself up for some larger construction jobs—how about laying the foundation for a small card castle

or some other dream house you could never afford? All the tools are included. You don't need a ruler, for instance, when you have a deck of cards. Nor do you need a calendar, for that matter! Don't believe me? Read on.

# Card Condo

**MATERIALS: 30 playing cards, the playing card box, and a textured hard surface**
**LEVEL: ♠ ♣ ♦ ♥**

How would you like to own a four-bedroom, two-story house with optional skylights and no money down? You already do. With about 30 cards, and a carpet or other hard, textured fiber surface (like a tableclothed table) for traction, all this can be yours!

**1.** Scope out a good piece of property. Remember that this is where your house will be, so choose a scenic spot (for those interested in a lake view, build near a pet's water bowl). Begin the house by constructing a "T" formation with cards: Hold two cards, resting on their sides, perpendicular to each other, touching at the end of one card and the middle of the other.

**2.** Add a third card to the opposite end, forming a capital letter "I". This is the foundation of your house and the most important part of the structure. And yes, neatness counts!

## CARD QUIZ

**How can you spot a marked deck?**

**The riffle test** probably originated on gambling riverboats in the 1800s, and it's still the best test for finding marks. Holding the deck facedown in your left hand, riffle the end of the deck upward like a flipbook. If the deck is marked, you'll see flowers, angels, and whatever else that has been altered come to life, as dots and blocked-out petals dance across the backs of the cards. Gamblers call this "going to the movies."

There exists another kind of marking, not detectable by the riffle test. "Juice" decks are a different marking system entirely, and one that is easier to spot from far away than with close inspection. The idea is to coat an area of a card with a faint trace of "juice," a diluted ink solution that casts a shadowy red or blue (depending on the color of the back design) over certain areas. Juice decks are used primarily so that a cheat can determine high cards from low cards.

**3.** Now knock these three cards over and repeat the process. I want you to get used to what it feels like to start over. Doubtless this will happen several times during the coming steps—remember, you are building a house with cards.

**4.** Repeat Steps 1 and 2, then simultaneously prop two cards against each end of the "I" base. By propping the cards opposite each other at the same time, there is a balance, which lessens your chance of knocking the structure over.

**5.** Prop two more cards against the other end of the "I" base, again applying them simultaneously to keep the structure balanced.

**6.** Modify one side of the structure by creating a gap between two of the cards, as shown: This will be your front door.

*Continued*

**7.** Enclose the structure by adding two cards to each side of the house, perpendicular to the front door. Looking into the house, you can see the division of rooms. The large room directly to the right makes an excellent master bedroom, and I can see an earth-tone theme working well in the dining room.

**8.** . . . And don't you just love that storage space to the left? Now you'll construct a nine-card roof. Start by laying three cards horizontally across the top of one side, as shown.

**9.** Lay three cards across the center, and finally three cards across the other side. Skylights really make the most of your property's natural light. If this interests you, just leave a gap in your thatching.

**10.** For the second story, you'll use the card box as a secret support system. Yes, card castle purists would frown on this infraction, but forge on. Balance the closed box on its side directly on top of your original "I" formation, which is the house's strongest point.

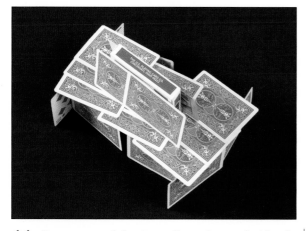

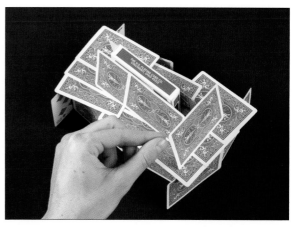

**11.** Lean two cards horizontally against each side of the card box.

**12.** Then lean one card horizontally against each end of the card box.

**13.** Finally, place two cards flat on top, covering the surface of the card box from view (just in case the purist drives his station wagon through your neighborhood). Enjoy your two-story dream house—just don't sneeze.

## MAPS AND CARDS

In 1590s England, "instructive" playing cards began to appear. The backs of these decks featured information on history, geography, mathematics, science, and grammar. The idea was simple: One would learn *as* he played.

The earliest reference to geography cards depicts regions of England and Wales on the face of each card, with traditional suits replaced with North, South, East, and West. In the seventeenth century, it is said that geographical cards like these were used by barons on the Isle of Man during competitive gambling. The stakes? The very lands depicted on the cards!

# Card Calendar

**MATERIALS: A deck of playing cards**     **LEVEL:** ♠ ♣ ♦ ♥

**W**hile a deck of cards is a well-known way to pass the time, you can also *keep* time with one. You can track every day of the year (including leap year, if you saved the Jokers) with one deck of cards. This system was developed by Professor Morgan Worthy of Georgia State University, who discovered the pattern while studying an Aztec calendar based on the same concept. Here's how:

**1.** Deal one card into a pile every day. On January 1, 2, 3, and 4, deal the cards into a pile facedown. That's important and standard. Every time you start with a full deck, the first four days (and cards) must be dealt facedown.

**2.** Every subsequent card is dealt faceup. When the pack is exhausted, 52 days have passed.

**3.** On the 53rd day, pick up all the faceup cards (48 cards) and repeat the procedure, dealing the first four cards/days facedown.

**4.** Deal the remaining cards faceup. Forty-eight days later (100 days, total, have passed), gather all the faceup cards and repeat.

**5.** Continue this process until no more faceup cards remain. You started with 52 days, then 48, then 44, and so on. The pattern looks like this: 52+48+44+40+36+32+28+24+20+16+12+8+4=364. When you've finished the cycle, the next day will be exactly a year from when you started. On normal years, deal a Joker on this day. For leap year, a second Joker is used to bring the count to 366 days.

## CARD QUIZ

**Can cards tell time?**

There are tall tales about cards that represent or are able to tell time, but there isn't any substantiating evidence to prove this. Still, the coincidences are staggering:

- Four seasons in a year and four suits in a deck.
- 13 lunar cycles of the moon and 13 cards in each suit.
- 52 weeks in a year and 52 cards in a deck. Also, if you count and add all the letters in the names of the 13 values (A-C-E is 3 plus T-W-O is 3 equals 6, and so on), the sum is exactly 52. (And, it even works in French.)
- 365 days in one year. If you add up the value of every card in the deck (11 for Jacks, 12 for Queens, 13 for Kings), the result is 364 . . . now add one for the Joker (the additional Joker is for use during leap years).

# Fortune-Telling

**MATERIALS: A deck of playing cards        LEVEL: ♠ ♣ ♦ ♥**

If you approached a tarot reader on the street and asked her about the cosmic meaning of playing cards, she would tell you that playing cards evolved from the numbered cards in the tarot pack (and she would probably also charge you a dollar for that answer). She would explain that gypsies brought the tarot to Europe in the 16th century and discovered ways to uncover a person's fate with a deal of the cards.

Fortune telling (called "cartomancy" with a regular pack) is, of course, a pack of lies generated by random shuffling, false prophecies, and generalities that could apply to anyone. It is almost certain that tarot cards evolved *from* playing cards, not the other way around. Here, I've outlined some standard "meanings" for playing cards. Just shuffle your deck, choose three cards, and let the false sense of fate run rampant.

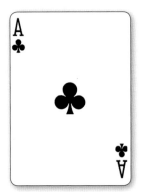

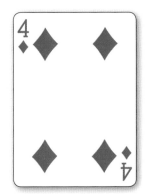

**Ace:** New beginnings, perhaps a new love or baby, increase in finances

**Two:** Torn between two choices, stability, starting fresh

**Three:** Creativity, communication, enlisting the aid of others

**Four:** Reevaluate your personal values, lover's quarrel, establishing a new home base

**Five:** Restlessness, changes, petty arguments, change of an opinion

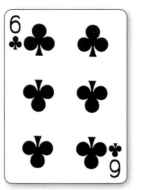

**Six:** Creativity, communication, three is a crowd, change directions

**Seven:** Harmony, adaptation, holding on to the past

**Eight:** Surprises, consistent effort eventually pays off, yes

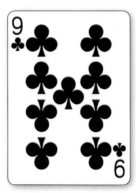

**Nine:** Surprises, unrealistic expectations, write the love letter

**Ten:** Karma, fear of leaving, follow the dream

**Jack:** Youth, mischief, don't judge before you try

**Queen:** Organized, efficient, maternal instincts

**King:** Entrepreneur, sincere, absolute conviction is necessary

## NOT ALL TAROT CARDS ARE CREATED EQUAL

Tarot decks come in many forms and sizes, but few are as desirable as Aleister Crowley's iteration, pictured here. Crowley was a turn-of-the-century occultist and hedonist who pioneered many alternative ceremonies. Crowley's pack uses imagery from many disciplines, and the artwork makes this deck collectable in tarot-reading circles.

# Card Box Balance

**MATERIALS: A deck of playing cards, the card box**     LEVEL: ♠ ♣ ♦ ♥

Iᵀt's the little things that bug me: hotel curtains that don't close all the way, the fact that my airplane seat has to be in an upright position when we land, furniture that wobbles. While a deck of cards won't help change hotel decor or flight regulations, it *is* the ideal solution for wobbly tables and chairs.

Sitting in a chair with one short leg is aggravating; every minor shift in weight is amplified by the chair's teeter-tottering. If there is a book around, you could potentially stick it under the short leg in hopes of leveling it out. But the chance of finding a book of exactly the right width is rare. It's more likely that you'll just make the leg longer than the other three: That solves nothing. But a deck of cards is adjustable.

**1.** Figure out exactly how many cards you'll need to match the thickness of the gap, say 33. Place exactly 33 cards in the box and close the flap.

**2.** Slide the card box under the deficient leg.

**3.** The box will cave in to the level of the playing cards, giving you the perfect extension and a sturdy piece of furniture!

# Card Ruler

**MATERIALS: A deck of playing cards     LEVEL: ♠ ♣ ♦ ♥**

**W**ith your right hand, reach toward your right hip and remove the tape measure secured to your belt. You can retire this fashion faux pas because your trusty deck of cards can measure almost as well.

A standard poker-sized playing card is 3½ inches long and 2½ inches wide. Remembering these two dimensions, you can easily measure most household items. No, cards won't tell you how many millimeters to adjust the family portrait above the fireplace or how many more feet you need to make your football field regulation. But cards can give you a rough estimate on furniture, wall space, and other household measuring duties, especially when someone has misplaced the tape measure. Good-bye yardstick, hello *card*stick! Here are a few useful combinations.

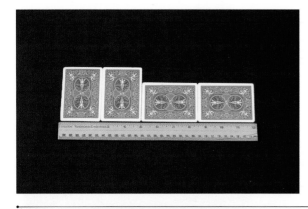

**1.** If you line up two cards widthwise (5 inches) and two cards lengthwise (7 inches), they will equal exactly one foot.

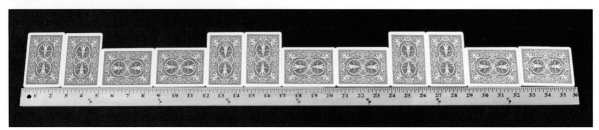

**2.** If you repeat the configuration in Step 1 three times, you'll have a sequence of cards that is equal to the length of a yard.

# CARD QUIZ

**How tall is the tallest house of cards?**

**More than 25 feet tall.** On October 14, 2007, Bryan Berg set the world record for the tallest house of cards: 120 stories (each story equals the height of one card). Berg's structures read more like magic tricks than stacking feats: a total of ten Guinness World Records plus other unbelievable projects, including a replica of the United States Capitol Building in Washington, D.C., and a structure that supported a team of Las Vegas showgirls (more than 2,700 pounds!).

Dallas, Texas, 2007: Guinness World Record by Bryan Berg for Tallest House of Freestanding Playing Cards.

**3.** Repeat the configuration in Step 2 five times and the line of cards equals 15 feet (and 60 cards). But to use just one deck, 50 cards lengthwise (175 inches) and two cards widthwise (5 inches) also yields exactly 15 feet.

# Card Calisthenics

MATERIALS: **A deck of playing cards**    LEVEL: ♠ ♣ ♦ ♥

**W**ho says sleight of hand is a passive hobby? I'm sure you think I'm kidding about this next game, but I'm not. The life of a magician is often a life of hotels, late nights, fast food, and boredom. Hence, this little challenge. This method of exercising makes 364 push-ups go quickly. If 364 push-ups are intimidating, switch the exercise to sit-ups. If 364 sit-ups are still too tough, switch to jumping jacks!

**1.** Place the deck facedown on the floor. Now lie down on your stomach, placing your hands palms down on the floor, just outside your shoulders. Bring your right hand to the pack of cards and slowly turn the top card faceup. Let's assume it's a Seven.

**2.** Immediately retract your right hand to its rest position, palm down on the carpet. You will now do *seven* push-ups, as indicated by the card. Now when I say push-up, I mean a real, chest-straining push-up. You'll practice only perfect form on my watch! Keep your body completely straight and your legs together.

**3.** When you're done, rest for a few seconds. Then turn over the next card.

**4.** Let's say fate has smiled on you this time and you've turned over the Two of Hearts. Do two more push-ups and take another rest. You're going to need it.

**5.** All told, you've got 364 push-ups in one pack of cards. Jacks are 11 push-ups, Queens are 12, and Kings, well . . . you'll feel the burn.

***Variation:*** As an alternative, you may wish to use tarot cards instead of playing cards. This way, you'll be exercising and *exorcising* at the same time!

## CARD ON FOREHEAD

Sometimes you just want to be left alone. And the next time you get that feeling, stick a card on your forehead. Nobody will want anything to do with you. I don't know where I first learned this or why it works, but the air-cushion finish on most playing cards makes them adhere to skin easily. And as you'll soon learn, walking down the street with the Three of Clubs on your face is a good way to ensure solitude.

If your skin is too dry for this to work, lick either the middle of your forehead or the back of the playing card—the end result is the same, but licking the card is easier. Press the center of the card firmly against the middle of your forehead and it should stick for a long time. The seal isn't strong, but using staples can be a little messy.

Where is the Queen? Finding the lady is not as easy as it seems: Don't fall for the "bent corner ruse," *page 184.*

# Chapter 7

# Safe Bets

**Suckers have no business with money anyway.**

—CANADA BILL JONES, *legendary 19th-century card hustler*

**C**ard counting takes months to master and gives the user only a 2-percent advantage at the blackjack table. A portable electronic device that calculates card

value probabilities based on information you input (with a toe switch) costs around $2,000, and 10 years of incarceration if caught. There *has* to be an easier way. And there are several, right here.

The following stunts are proven ways of separating a sucker from his money, and give you a 100-percent advantage. The layman's term for this is "cheating." Just remember: You didn't read these stunts here, you and I don't know each other, and this book doesn't exist.

In their treatise on card cheating, David Britland and Gazzo observe, "A deck of cards in the hands of a cheat is a weapon of unsurpassed criminal possibilities."

# According to Hoyle

**MATERIALS: A deck of playing cards**    **LEVEL:** ♠ ♣ ♦ ♥

**A**ccording to Hoyle and everyone else, a royal flush (Ten, Jack, Queen, King, and Ace of the same suit) ranks higher than four Aces, but winner can take all with these four Aces, thanks to a little-known scam, and some verbal misdirection.

**1.** Go up to the biggest poker hotshot you know and pose this challenge (make a wager on it if possible): "You can't beat four Aces with a royal flush."

**2.** Take your deck and remove four Aces for your hand. Now throw him the cards and ask him to remove his royal flush.

**3.** First he removes the Ten and Jack of Spades confidently.

**4.** There is hesitation as he tables the Queen of Spades, because he is slowly realizing what you've done. He shakes his head as he reveals the King of Spades and then he stops.

**5.** He can't remove the final card, the Ace of Spades, because you already have four Aces. Checkmate!

# HOLDOUT DEVICES

**T**his "Martin" holdout (below), circa 1890, deposits cards into the cheater's hands from his sleeve. A wire connected the device pictured to a pull, operated either between the knees or at the toes. The "Keplinger" holdout (inset) was the first device of its kind. It was sewn into the hem of the user's cuff and would deliver cards into the palm of the hand. This particular specimen was pulled off a corpse—a reminder of the dangers men who wore these devices could face if caught.

Cheaters have devised ways to hide cards virtually everywhere. This holdout device (above left and right) conceals desirable cards against the chest, and when the cheat spreads his knees beneath the card table, he triggers the device which releases the hidden cards between the buttons in his vest, and surreptitiously adds them to the hand he was dealt.

This deck-switching device (above left and right) is concealed in a most private area: the crotch. The unit is loaded with a "cooler" (the deck to be switched in) just beneath the waistband. Between rounds, the dealer casually rests one hand on his lap, drops the used pack into a gap in his pants waistband and takes the cooler from a protruding mechanical arm. The switch takes place in less than a second and out of the other players' view.

# Three's a Crowd

**MATERIALS: A deck of playing cards**      **LEVEL:** ♠ ♣ ♦ ♥

**P**ulling this stunt will make you feel like the rowdiest carny at the fair, and who hasn't wanted to be that guy at least once? Whether it's knocking over milk bottles or throwing Ping-Pong balls into a sea of goldfish, the end result is always the same: "That's harder than it looks."

**1.** Remove five picture cards and two number cards from the deck.

**2.** Display the cards, collect them facedown in your hand, and mix them. Then deal them facedown in a row.

**3.** Announce the bet, wagering that the spectator cannot pick three picture cards in a row. "The odds are always in your favor," you explain. "The first round you've got a 5 in 7 chance. That's like shooting fish in a barrel. It's practically guaranteed. The next time it's 4 out of 6—I just wish I had those odds in Vegas—I would be rich in a week. Last, the probability of choosing a picture card is 3 out of 5, which is still more than a fair shot. You can't afford *not* to make this bet."

**4.** The proposition seems logical enough, but it's tougher than it seems. While the odds of pulling a picture card in each individual round are correctly outlined in your pitch, the wager is based on three *consecutive* picture cards.

**5.** To correctly calculate the probability, you need to multiply the probability in each round: 5/7 times 4/6 times 3/5. If eighth-grade math wasn't your forte, the result is 2/7. So your opponent will be successful in only 28.6 percent of the cases, which makes you the winner a whopping 71.4 percent of the time.

# Flipped  ON DVD

**MATERIALS: A deck of playing cards, a table surface**     LEVEL: ♠ ♣ ♦ ♥

**M**any of the sleights and ruses that magicians use to dazzle were originally used to deceive. Flipped can be used to amaze or confound, depending on whether you present it as magic or a con. Below, you'll explore how best to exploit the principle as a bet. But fear not, you can't lose.

**CONCEALED VIEW**

**1.** Secretly note the bottom card of your deck—con men call this a "key" card.

**2.** Approach a guy with an obtuse look on his face—con men call guys like this "marks." Ask him to cut the cards and place the cut-off portion in your hand.

**3.** Ask him to remember the card he cut to, pointing to the packet on the table. Let's say it's the Two of Clubs.

**4.** Ask the mark to replace the card on top of the cards in your hand.

**5.** Then ask him to complete the cut by placing the tabled packet on top of everything. While it appears that the mark cut the deck, looked at a card, and then buried it, his selection actually rests just below the card you remembered at the outset. You have complete control over the card, and he hasn't got a clue.

**6.** Begin dealing the cards in a faceup pile, one by one. Instruct your participant not to indicate if you pass his card—you'll find it without any help. This is all smoke; you know exactly where his card is. You can deal with relative speed, all the while watching for the key card. When you deal the key card faceup, it's time to pay close attention.

**7.** Without breaking rhythm, deal the participant's selection faceup *and then two more cards.* You want to give the impression that you've unknowingly botched the demonstration.

*Continued* 👉

**8.** Take the next card facedown in the right hand and stare at it intently. "The next card I turn over will be your card. Do you want to wager against that?" The circumstances are extraordinary: The probability of actually finding the right card are 1 in 52. The mark has also seen his card come and go onto the pile of discards, so he can be sure the card in the right hand is not his—and it's not. He won't be able to get to his wallet fast enough.

**9.** Whatever he offers to bet, hesitate for a moment, as if it's too much, but ultimately agree to as much as he is willing to bet—at least the tab on your next drink. To win the bet, place the card in your right hand facedown on the table.

**10.** Spread over the top two indifferent cards on the discard pile, exposing the participant's selection.

**11.** Pick up the card so your participant can see, and turn it facedown.

**12.** You win, game over. Remind him that you said "The next card I turn over will be your card." The next card you turned over really was his card. Sometimes ambiguity pays off; it just paid for your drink.

## MISSING FINGER DEAL

**To be able to deal from the bottom requires long and continued practice. Very few are expert at it, and unless it is well done, it is well left alone.**

—Weasel Murphy, *The Professional Gambler's Handbook*

The dealer to the left appears legit, but look closer: He's only showing three fingers. The photo to the right shows a proper grip. Dealing cards from the bottom or "basement," however, is much easier if there are fewer fingers wrapped around the deck. The antiquated grip, left, called the missing finger deal, has been replaced by more modern grips, but it remains the most infamous to date, mostly because of the lengths its users were willing to go. On 19th-century riverboats, where poker and cheating at poker were both in their infancy, trust among players was harder to come by. A missing finger during the deal could earn you a bullet in the gut. Some dedicated cheats even severed the middle finger of their left hands so that only four digits were ever present, deal or no deal.

# Joker Is on You!

**MATERIALS: A Joker, 14 other playing cards, a table surface**   LEVEL: ♠ ♣ ♦ ♥

This game seems like even odds, but if you know the secret, you can't lose. The key to winning (what, you thought I'd leave you hanging?) is remembering the numbers 13, 9, and 5. You can commit these to memory using this handy mnemonic I devised (sung to the tune of "Happy Birthday"): "Thir-teen nine then five, thir-teen nine then five, thir-teen nine then fi-ive, thir-teen nine then five." The objective is simple: Don't get left with the Joker. In order to avoid this, you must leave your opponent with 13, 9, or 5 cards after each turn.

**1.** Holding the packet of cards, separate the Joker and show it to your opponent. Then place it faceup on the table.

**2.** Place the other 14 cards squared on top. Present the challenge: Alternating turns, you are each allowed to remove one, two, or three cards from the pile until it is exhausted. The person left with the Joker at the end of the game loses.

**3.** Suppose your opponent goes first and she takes away one card. Your total is now 14 cards in the pile. In order to get to 13 when she moves again, you'll need to remove just one card.

***Troubleshooting:*** Occasionally if your opponent goes first, she may remove three cards, which means you cannot reach your first objective of 13. However, you can continue the game unflustered, because you can still reach the next total, 9, by removing the proper amount of cards.

**4.** Out of the pile of 13 cards, perhaps she removes 2, leaving 11 cards in the pile. To get to nine (the second remembered number), you'll need to remove two cards.

**5.** She then removes three, leaving six cards in the pile. You'll remove one card to bring the total to five.

**6.** Once five cards remain, you have won.

**7.** She can remove one, two, or three cards from the five-card pile, but you'll still be able to remove all the cards except for one . . . the Joker of doom.

## CARD QUIZ

**What role did cards play in the emancipation of Texas?**

**When most people think of the Alamo and Texas's emancipation from Mexico,** they think of Davy Crockett, Jim Bowie, or perhaps Ozzy Osbourne. I think of playing cards. Here's why: Just after the fall of the Alamo, General Sam Houston led Texas to freedom at the battle of San Jacinto. This campaign involved Mexicans on *both* sides; some Mexicans fought alongside Texans to liberate the state, while the Mexican army fought to maintain control of the land. To differentiate the Mexican-Americans from the Mexican-Mexicans, General Houston instructed all the Mexican-Americans to place playing cards in their hats. So if you saw someone with the Seven of Clubs sticking out of his brim, you would not shoot! He was on our side.

# Throwing Cards Into a Hat

**MATERIALS: A deck of playing cards, a hat**     LEVEL: ♠ ♣ ♦ ♥

**P**eople say throwing cards into a hat is a piece of cake. Properties of playing cards, however, are not easily understood. A simple task like dropping cards into a hat is actually almost impossible unless you know the secret. This next game is one you can't lose.

**1.** The first step is to borrow a hat and place it on the floor. In lieu of a fedora, use a sports cap or bowl.

**2.** Explain that the task is to drop the cards from waist height into the hat. As you explain the stunt, gesture with a playing card by holding it perpendicular to the floor, so that when you look down at the card you see only its edge.

**3.** Separate 20 cards from the deck. Hand the participant (your opponent) 10 cards and take 10 for yourself. Explain the challenge: The person with the most cards in the hat wins.

**4.** Your opponent goes first. She will invariably drop the cards from a perpendicular position, as you demonstrated, which results in the card fluttering out of line and away from the hat. It's likely your opponent won't get any cards into the hat.

**5.** The secret of this game is to drop the cards on a horizontal plane, parallel with the floor.

**6.** By doing this, the card will fall straight down, directly into the hat.

# Stepping Through a Card

**MATERIALS: One playing card, a pair of scissors**    LEVEL: ♠♣♦♥

"**I**'ll bet you I can cut a hole in a playing card big enough to step through." By now, your friends should know better than to accept this wager. But there are still many who would bet against you, so grab some scissors and follow along. You'll destroy a card with this stunt, rendering the rest of the deck incomplete, so unless you have a deck to spare, try this with the joker or one of the other spare cards in the box.

**2.** Fold the card widthwise, short end to short end, with the back design facing out. There are now two ends on this folded card: the open end and the folded end.

**1.** "I'll bet you I can cut a hole in this playing card that's big enough to step through," you announce.

**3.** To make a hole big enough to step through, you'll make a series of small cuts, alternating from the folded end and the open end. Holding the folded end nearest the body, make a cut about ⅛ inch from the right side edge, *stopping* about 3/16 inch before you reach the open end.

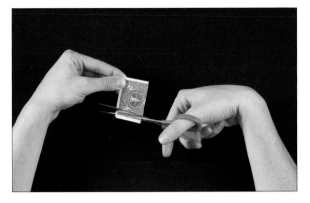

**4.** Turn the folded card 180 degrees, so that the open end is nearest the body and the slit is now on the card's far left. Cut ⅛ inch to the right of the first cut, again stopping just before you reach the end of the folded card.

**5.** Rotate the card back 180 degrees and make the next cut, ⅛ inch away, and parallel to the first.

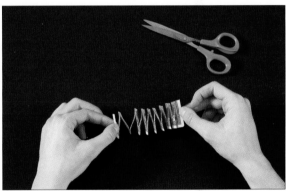

**6.** Continue rotating the card and cutting until the pattern covers the entire folded card. *Note:* The last cut must originate at the folded side (matching the first cut into the card).

**7.** The folded playing card should resemble the card shown here.

*Continued* 👉

**8.** Carefully unfold the card.

**9.** Without cutting the rightmost and leftmost card strips of the card, use your scissors to bisect the card at the fold, as shown.

**10.** You must *not* cut the first or last piece.

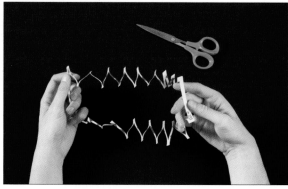

**11.** Gently extend the edges of the card, revealing a "hoop" of sorts.

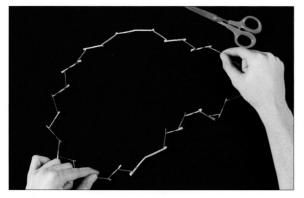

**12.** To stretch out the hoop, flatten the "joints" by pinching them between your fingers.

**13.** Step through the hoop! How far through the card you're able to step depends on your size and how close together you made the cuts in Steps 3–6. I have really big feet, but I can cut strips thin enough to step inside the card every time. *Note:* If you're slight, you may even be able to step through the entire card! If you can't get the framework around your shoulders (I can't), you can still bank on being able to at least "step through" a hole you can cut out of one playing card, which is enough to win the wager.

# Flicked

MATERIALS: **One playing card, a coin**    LEVEL: ♠ ♣ ♦ ♡

If you've ever fantasized about whisking a tablecloth out from under a full table setting, this stunt is a gratifying (and less risky) substitute. Removing a card from one's finger without disturbing the coin resting on top is not impossible, but it is difficult unless you know the secret.

**1.** Present a coin (a nickel or a quarter work well) and a playing card to a participant.

**2.** Place the card (faceup or facedown, it doesn't matter) on his finger pad and balance the coin on top. Challenge him to remove the card while leaving the coin balanced on the tip of his finger . . . without touching the coin.

**3.** Once your participant has failed, set up the coin and card on your own fingertip, then simply flick the edge of the card, with force.

**4.** The card will fly away, leaving the coin (which you did *not* touch) balanced on your fingertip.

# Three-Card Monte

**MATERIALS: The Queen of Hearts, two black cards, and a cardboard box**

**LEVEL:** ♠ ♣ ♦ ♥

Watching a game of three-card monte can be riveting. Here are some equally riveting facts about three-card monte:

1. You can never win.

2. This is not a game of skill or speed; you are being cheated.

3. The monte "tosser" rarely works alone. The consistent winners are friends or relatives of the tosser.

4. You can never, never, *never* win.

In prison, the going rate for the information you're about to learn is $500. You see, behind bars is often where criminals become con men. Then again, behind bars is where con men often end up. Let's end our exploration into playing cards with this, the most notorious scam of them all.

It begins like this: Three-card monte is a mesmerizing game with seemingly enticing odds.

**Hi diddle diddle,**

**The Queen is in the middle.**

**When the money goes down,**

**The lady can't be found!**

**Red you choose,**

**Black you lose!**

**You bet too fast,**

**You never last.**

**You bet too slow,**

**You got to go.**

—Frank Garcia's classic monte pitch,
*Don't Bet on It*

**1.** The tosser displays three cards over a cardboard box: two black cards and the Queen of Hearts.

Continued ☞

**2.** The cards are always bent in a convex-tent shape so that they are easier to hold. Since the cards will be tossed over one another, an all-over back design is favored over a bordered back design. With an all-over back design, it is harder to follow the cards as they are mixed.

**3.** The three cards are placed face down on the box surface. Your task as a spectator is simple: Find the lady. But as the tosser turns the cards facedown and mixes them, more is going on than meets the eye.

**4.** To mix the cards, the tosser will usually take one card by the ends in the left hand and the other two cards in the right hand, stacked.

## CARD QUIZ

**Are cards illegal?**

**Today, if you are caught _cheating_ at cards you might end up in jail,** but 500 years ago, merely _playing_ cards was against the law in most places. When cards began to spread across Europe in the 14th century, gambling, drunkenness, and fighting followed closely. As a result, our beloved pasteboards got a bad rap.

In 1376, the city of Florence enacted the first edict against gaming, and in 1423, St. Bernardino of Sienna preached against the use of playing cards and held a public card-burning in Bologna. Sixteenth-century Brits were slightly more lenient; playing cards was forbidden except during the 12 days of Christmas. And apparently, some feared playing cards would lead to infidelity. In 1576, John Northbrooke wrote a pamphlet attributing the invention of cards to Satan, adding "that he might the easier bring in Ydolatrie among men."

**5.** He will throw the cards to the box's surface in rapid succession, but there's an added variable: the toss. The toss is gambler's jargon for a secret move that has cost honest people their Saturday stash for more than a hundred years. The tosser holds two cards in his right hand, and you can never be sure which one he is throwing. *Example:* The tosser picks up a black card in his right hand and flashes its face to you.

**6.** With the same hand, he now takes the money card, the Queen of Hearts. Once again, he flashes its identity to reel in the players.

**7.** When he executes the toss, it will appear as if he throws the Queen onto his working surface. Actually, he releases the upper, indifferent card. This card comes shooting out of the right hand and lands facedown, disguised as the Queen. Every pair of eyes on that street corner, including yours, is now locked on this indifferent card, and after some easy-to-follow mixing, the Queen is revealed elsewhere, and you're 20 bucks poorer.

# ઌ THE BENT CORNER RUSE ૭

**"It hardly takes much intelligence to realize you can't make a profit in any game where the house only accepts losing wagers."**

—DARWIN ORTIZ, *Gambling Scams*

It's time to introduce the cast and characters for the three-card monte. You already know the star of the show, the "broad tosser." This is the guy who actually does all the secret moves and orchestrates the pace of the game. Being called a broad tosser doesn't mean he's been on Jerry Springer; it's an expression coined from a slang synonym for a playing card. Now meet the wallman and the shills.

The "wallman" is the quiet, unsuspecting guy leaning against the corner building. He's a lookout and will signal the tosser if police approach. The "shills" breathe life into three-card monte. They are undercover grifters who are there to make suckers jealous by winning so much easy money. "Hey," the shill says, "I can find the Queen, too."

You can always pick out the shills at three-card monte because only the shills win. The tosser has both visual and auditory cues for the shills, telling them the exact position of the elusive Queen. The tosser will accept only losing wagers from passersby. If, by a stroke of luck, a stranger puts down 50 bucks on the right card, a shill will bet twice as much on the same card. Oh, and one more rule the tosser didn't mention until now . . . he only takes the biggest bet. The shill wins again.

The shill and the tosser work together for the most devious ruse of all: the bent corner.

**1.** Between games, while the tosser is collecting money, one of the players will secretly reach onto the cardboard box and bend the corner of the Queen, rendering it completely identifiable. The tosser didn't notice, but a curious soccer mom, shopping bag in hand, noticed—and she's already reaching for her wallet.

The tosser pretends not to notice the glaring crimp in the Queen.

1.

**2.**

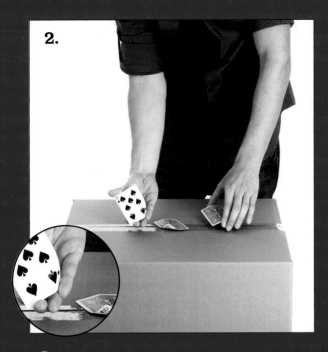

**3.**

**2.** Still, he begins to mix the cards as if nothing has changed. As he mixes the cards, however, he is executing a deft maneuver imperceptible to viewers. First, the tosser will secretly bend the corner of one of the black cards with his little finger. Since everyone's attention is focused on the facedown Queen, this goes unnoticed. All three of the cards have "soft" corners, meaning before the game the tosser gently bent all the corners back and forth, making them more pliable; with soft cards, the crimps are just as easy to remove as they are to put in.

**3.** After executing the toss, switching in the bent black card and retaining the Queen in the hand, the tosser will remove the crimp from the Queen with his little finger and then toss it back to the table. In a matter of seconds, the bent Queen is gone, and so is the soccer mom's money.

## CARD QUIZ

**Who is Canada Bill?**
**Canada Bill (center) is the most famous tosser of all time.**
He made impressive amounts of money off railroad travelers during the 1870s. It was so lucrative that he wrote to the officials of the Union Pacific Railroad. He offered the company an annual fee of $10,000 for the right to play three-card monte hassle-free on the trains. As part of the deal, he promised to cheat only Chicago commercial travelers and Methodist priests. Go figure—the deal didn't fly.

A very crooked deal.

# Last Words

**Playing cards are a survival of our less rational, more frightful, more beautiful past.**

—David Mamet, in *Playing Cards* by Donald Sultan

**W**hen I look at playing cards, I see limitless potential. When these simple symbols are shuffled, fortunes are won, the future is foretold, or magic is unleashed.

Cards can be used for self-defense or to separate a sucker from his money. They personify our innate obsession with chance, and they reward our strategic cunning. The cards themselves are relics of ancient times and craft, and their history is forever intertwined with ours. Whether it's the World Series of Poker or a child seeing his first magic trick, lives can change with the turn of a card. I've enjoyed sharing my quirky collection of "cardistry" with you, and I hope these stunts are as fun for you to do as they have been for me to invent, practice, and describe. Playing cards are my obsession; they have taken me all over the world and exposed me to fascinating people and unforgettable experiences. For these reasons and more, I'm equally indebted to the cards and to you.

Take care, and take cards.

— JOSHUA JAY
*New York City*

# CARD QUIZ

**How many eyes are on a deck of cards?**

**If you said 42, 48, 739, or "Who cares," you're correct.** When asked this question, most people incorrectly assume eyes are found only on the faces of the court figures. Since there are 12 court cards (four Jacks, four Queens, and four Kings), the logical answer would be 24. But don't forget there are two one-eyed Jacks and a one-eyed King of Diamonds (in a Bicycle deck, anyway). Further, don't forget that playing cards are nondirectional, so there are two heads, one on each end of the card. Thus, the King of Hearts has four eyes, two on each head. This brings our running total to 42 (four eyes on each court card except the Jacks of Hearts and Spades and the King of Diamonds, which have only two).

But there's more. The Ace of Spades in most decks, including Bicycle, has a figure of a lady inside the Spade pip. Add two. Two Jokers are technically part of a "deck of cards," and each Joker has two eyes, so add four more. Our running total is now 48.

Since playing cards have a front and a back, we can't ignore the back designs. Bicycle's trademark is the angel-on-bicycle image, but there are a total of six angels on the back of every Bicycle rider back design. The total number of eyes (and nipples, for the curious) on the back of Bicycle cards is 648. That brings us to 696 . . . but there's more.

If you're posing this problem verbally, you never distinguish an "E-Y-E" from the letter "I". If you count the letter "I" and the part of the facial anatomy of the same name together, the grand total is 719 (5 "I"s on the Ace of Spades and 18 on the Joker).

# Appendix

## Further Reading

The world of playing cards is fragmented, but it is full of generous, inventive people. The only prerequisite for participating in any of these organizations is a love for playing cards and the ability to do eight perfect one-handed faro shuffles. I'm kidding about that last part.

## For Card Tricks

If you liked the card tricks and flourishes in the pages of this book, let me make three recommendations to you.

**1.** Join a magic society. There's no better path to becoming a great magician than joining a fraternal organization. Magicians meet for lectures, conventions, and monthly gatherings (these are not as dorky as they sound; in fact, they're quite fun). The two biggest U.S.-based magic organizations are:

 The International Brotherhood of Magicians www.magician.org

The Society of American Magicians www.magicsam.com

**2.** Check out *Magic: The Complete Course,* written by me, and brought to you by the same kind folks who published the book and DVD you're holding. This is the magic book and DVD I wish I'd had

when I started. It's equal parts presentation and technique, and between the covers are over a hundred professional-caliber magic tricks you can do. For card lovers, there's a chapter called "The Ten Greatest Card Tricks of All Time."

**3.** If you like flourishes (fans, fancy cuts, etc.), check out www.dananddave.com. Dan and Dave Buck are twins who have, in essence, started a new movement with card flourishes. These guys shuffle cards with superhuman agility, and they have a burgeoning online community to support this creative and exciting new trend.

## For Card History

If playing-card history or collecting is your thing, allow me to make three more suggestions:

**1.** Join the International Playing-Card Society. Based in the U.K. but with membership all over the world, this is the best way to learn about the history of playing cards and how to view the best collections all over the world. http://i-p-c-s.org

**2.** Next time you're in Paris, visit *Le Musée Français de la Carte à Jouer,* a stunning museum with an unrivaled display of cards of every shape and design.

You'll have a new appreciation for cards as works of art. www.issy.com/statiques/musee/

**3.** Read *Roll the Bones: The History of Gambling* by David G. Schwartz. This is a much overdue modern tome on the colorful history of gambling. It also covers the most modern developments concerning the origins of playing cards.

Playing-Card History: Playing cards have a rich history and industry, yet there is no generally accepted consensus on some of the most fundamental questions. The brief glimpses into the origins and trivia of playing cards have been gleaned from numerous sources, people, and experiences. Some notable titles:

*A History of Playing Cards and a Bibliography of Cards and Gaming,* by Catherine Perry Hargrave, 1930, Dover Reprint Edition.

## For Cheaters and Cons

Finally, for those of you fascinated by the underworld of cheaters, mechanics, con men, and advantage play, here are three exhilarating *true* tales that center around a pack of cards:

**1.** *The Magician and the Cardsharp* by Karl Johnson, 2005, Henry Holt Books. This book chronicles the obsession of magic's greatest card expert, Dai Vernon. He became obsessed with the elusive center deal sleight and its fabled practitioner. His journey eventually brought him to the unlikeliest of places and the sketchiest of cheaters.

**2.** *Phantoms of the Card Table* by David Britland and Gazzo, 2003, High Stakes Publishing. This book, which also deals with Dai Vernon (it's hard to write about the subject *without* including the guy), surveys many of the most colorful characters who shuffled cards, and also the techniques themselves.

**3.** *Road Hustler* by Robert C. Prus and C.R.D. Sharper, 1977, expanded edition published by Kaufman and Greenberg. Hard to find but invaluable to the serious student, this is a close analysis of a real (and anonymous) card cheat. Not only are techniques discussed, but this book delves into the psychology of establishing trust, and even deeper into the psyche of the cheat.

# Acknowledgments

All of the following people have two things in common. All of them provided invaluable assistance on this project. And at one time or another, each of them picked a card (and I'm happy to report that in all cases, I found the right one). Thanks, everyone, for watching my tricks and helping make this book what it is.

*Joshua Jay's Amazing Book of Cards* has been six years in the making. I wrote the first draft in 2003 in France, where I had access to some of the finest card magicians in the world and the world's largest playing card museum. Thanks to Bebel and Sebastien Clergue for early inspiration, and to *Le Musée Français de la Carte à Jouer* for letting me stay late and touch stuff I wasn't supposed to. Thanks also to playing card experts Tom and Judy Dawson and Cláudio Décourt for answering a few important questions.

A very early draft of this book became my senior thesis; my gratitude to Michelle Herman, my thesis advisor (and favorite professor), and Cameron Filipour and Christopher Coake.

I am ever indebted to my brain trust and most cherished readers: Rod Doiron, Jason England, Trisha

Ferruccio, Joel Givens, Andi Gladwin, Raj Madhok, Jim Munsey, and Tyler Wilson.

Special thanks to Max Maven for his expertise in so many areas, and for his friendship. And to Jason England, whose knowledge of gambling history is incredible.

Eric Anderson and I collaborated on the breathtaking ephemera photos throughout the book, and I thank him for his excellent work. We spent many long hours photographing fascinating and rare cheating equipment, and I offer thanks to Doug Edwards and Simon Lovell, who generously made their valuable, fragile collections available to us. Thanks also to "Mr. M.," another friend who loaned me two rare pieces that appear in these pages—as promised, he shall remain anonymous.

This book wouldn't be in your hands if not for the enthusiastic support of James Levine, Suzie Bolotin, and Peter Workman. Many thanks to Megan Nicolay, my editor and friend, who is becoming scary-good with a pack of cards. And to the rest of the team at Workman: Anne Kerman, Janet Vicario, Julie Duquet, Tom Boyce, Kristin Matthews, Selina Meere, and many others. And for support with the photo shoot: Kristin Folk, Cristina Pandrea, Christine Choe, Nate Lifton, and Liz Davis.

To my management team, James Diener, Randy Jackson, and Charlie Walk: You have all my gratitude for believing in me and helping me achieve my dreams.

Thanks to my family, who have endured more card tricks than anyone alive: The Martuccios, the Cohens, Rocco Ferruccio, David Jay, and Patricia Michaels. And to my mom, for her unbounded support for everything important to me.

# Credits

## CHAPTER 1
## ALL HANDS ON DECK

The topics of this chapter—spreads, fans, flourishes—are always popular with card handlers. The originators of these techniques are unknown except where otherwise noted. The One-Handed Fan technique was taught to me personally by magician Bob Rees. His method is otherwise unpublished.

Ricky Jay, one-time world record–holder and accomplished sleight-of-hand artist, authored the definitive book on throwing cards, *Cards as Weapons*, 1977, Darien Books.

My other sources included:

*Card Manipulations* and *More Card Manipulations* by Jean Hugard, 1934–36, republished by Dover.

*Expert Card Technique* by Jean Hugard and Frederick Braue, 1940, republished by Dover.

*Slithering Snakes and Slick Spreads: National Geographic* article by Jeremy Berlin, March 2010, page 26.

Electric Deck: In 1868, Robert-Houdin described a strung-together deck, a precursor to the modern "Electric Deck" (a title first coined by Conradi in 1868).

"Where do playing cards come from?": Playing cards were (and often still are) different from region to region. Suits are sometimes made up of coins, batons, swords, cups, acorns, bells, or leaves. And even the amount of cards in packs vary: In Italy and Spain, many decks consist of only 32 cards.

See W. Benham Gurney, *Playing Cards: The History and Secrets of the Pack*, Spring Books, London, date unknown, p. 1.

"Where did the expression 'Not playing with a full deck' come from?": In 1628 the English Government established the Worshipful Company of Makers of Playing Cards to combat the foreign brands that dominated the marketplace. The company still exists today and is the premiere British manufacturer of cards. One of my favorite provisions from their constitution: No person using the trade may teach the trade or reveal "any of the secrets, skill, or misterys of the said Art or Trade" to anyone not a freeman of the company. The idea, of course, was to keep the manufacture of playing cards for British people within the borders of Britain.

See W. Benham Gurney, *Playing Cards: The History and Secrets of the Pack,* Spring Books, London, date unknown, p. 60.

## CHAPTER 2
## TRICKS

The Card Shark: The general concept of this effect was invented by V. F. Grant in 1932.

One Ahead: This classic card effect was first printed by Horatio Galasso in 1593. And it remains one of the most effective principles in card magic. I came across this effect in *Gibecière,* Vol. 2, No. 2, which is a complete translation of Galasso's original *Giochi di Carte Bellissimi.*

The Ten-Twenty Force: Also known as the Count-Back Force, the earliest version in print is likely by Billy O'Connor in the *Magic Wand* in 1935. Henry DeMuth has also been historically linked to this force.

Barely Lift a Finger: This is "Impromptu Haunted Deck" by Bert Fenn. See *Pallbearer's Review,* January 1974, p. 704. It is based on a principle in Charles Jordan's "The Deck That Cuts Itself" from *Thirty Card Mysteries* (1919).

Friction Four: Retaining the top and bottom cards in each hand while throwing goes back to master card expert Johann Hofzinser's "The Four Eights" in *Kartenkünste* (1910, English translation 1931), written by Ottokar Fischer and translated into English by S. H. Sharpe.

"How are playing cards made?": See Leo Behnke, *The Making of Playing Cards,* Lybrary.com edition, 2005, p. 9.

"How many decks of cards are printed each year?": Statistics compiled and published by Leo Behnke. See *The Making of Playing Cards,* Lybrary.com edition, 2005, p. 3.

"What is the Solitaire Encryption Algorithm (and is it part of our homework)?": The idea for coding a message around the edges of a pack of cards was explained to me by Martin Gardner. Historian Vanni Bossi traced the code back to 1563 in *De Furtivis Literarum Notis, Vulgo de Ziferis,* by Giovan Battista Della Porta. Bossi's findings were published in the Winter, 2005 issue of *Gibecière* (Vol. 1, No. 1).

Theodore Annemann mentioned the idea of writing on the side of the deck. Winston Freer was probably the first to use it in a trick with his "Half-wit Deck" with patter by Gene Gordon (who also marketed it). The first to apply it to a trick related to Paul Gertner's later "Unshuffled" was Hen Fetsch, in *The Linking Ring,* Jan. 1948, under the title "Mixed Magic."

## CHAPTER 3
## SHUFFLE BORED

The chapter title is a play on words coined by my esteemed friend and fellow magician Simon Aronson, who used the title for an inspiring card trick and booklet in 1980, and then collected it in *Bound to Please,* 1994.

Hindu Shuffle: The Hindu appellation comes from Jean Hugard who introduced it in the first volume of his *Card Manipulations* in 1934, but the shuffle itself predates this.

Tabled Riffle Shuffle: Martin Nash passed away in 2009, and he was most supportive of this project. He was kind to me in my formative years, and it was with great sadness that I changed the passage about him from present to past tense.

Overhand Shuffle: This shuffle goes back at least as far as 1584. We know this because Reginald Scot describes how to cheat using this shuffle in his

*Discoverie of Witchcraft*, arguably the first book containing card tricks in the English language.

Faro Shuffle: The first execution of a one-handed Faro Shuffle was likely by Howard de Courcy, in the early 1940s. Colleague Tyler Wilson has this to say about the origins of the faro shuffle: "The idea of perfectly interweaving cards during a shuffle—such as in a faro shuffle—was published in *The Whole Art and Mystery of Modern Gaming Fully Expos'd and Detected; Containing An Historical Account Of all the Secret Abuses Practis'd in the Game of Chance* (1726), written by an anonymous author who refers to himself only as 'Your Lordship's Most obliged and most obedient humble Servant.'"

Double Bridge: This technique is credited to Andreas Edmüller (*Card College*, Vol. 4, p. 1017). Steve Beam was the first to publish a controlled separation after the bridge.

*Really* Shuffle the Cards: See Diaconis, Persi, and Dave Bayer, *Trailing the Dovetail Shuffle to Its Lair, Annals of Applied Probability*, Vol. 2, No. 2, 1992, pp. 294–313. There is now competing literature that refutes these results: see L. N. Trefethen and L. M. Trefethen, *Proceedings: Mathematical, Physical, and Engineering Sciences*, Vol. 456, No. 2002 (Oct. 8, 2000), pp. 2561–2568.

The inefficiency of the Riffle Shuffle was first discussed by C. O. Williams around the turn of the century. Further exploration was made by Charles Jordan, who published a number of clever applications in the first quarter of the 20th century.

False Cut: Jay Ose popularized this clever, counterintuitive ruse. See Harry Lorayne, *Close-Up Card Magic*, 1962, p. 93. Its progenitor is Richard Himber's False Cut, published in *The Tarbell System* in 1926. Magician and historian Roberto Giobbi has managed to track the cut back to 1896: Conradi-Horster published "Falsches Mischen" in his book, *Der Moderne Kartenkünstler*.

"Shuffling cards is cool. But what is *un*-shuffling?": The world record for card sorting is organized annually by the German Association of Mind Training. See www.recordholders.org/en/records/cardsorting.html

Information on the prison card-sorting program can be found on the Warm Springs Correctional Center: www.doc.nv.gov/?q=node/31. David Pepka pointed out this prison program to me; he insists his knowledge of it is not from experience.

# CHAPTER 4
# CARDS AND CRAFTS

This chapter is a potpourri of projects that alter playing cards for one reason or another.

Leap Frog: This is a standard origami fold adapted to playing cards by Michael Close, for use in a magic trick. See "The Frog Prince," *Workers, Volume 2*, 1991.

Cards in a Bottle: I learned this technique from Harry Eng (see "Eng's Bottles," *Art of Astonishment, Book 2*, 1996, p. 303). Harry was an amazing guy; he made impossible bottles of every sort: some had baseballs, blocks of wood, and scissors. And, of course, cards.

Playing Card Wallet: Peter Rubinstein has kindly allowed me to adapt his playing card wallet design and describe my own iteration here.

Playing Card Purse: Ms. Hope King provided the plans for this playing card purse, and I'm grateful to her for allowing me to describe it here.

Wow Cards: Rowland's work in this area owes much to Robert Neale's seminal "Trapdoor Card" and its variations.

Marking Cards: Marked playing cards are a sinister, logical outgrowth of cards themselves, and date back nearly as far. The first mention of marked cards appears in 1408, in a letter housed in the French National Archives. The letter chronicles a scam perpetrated with marked cards by one Colin Charles. The first printed account of marked cards occurs in 1520 in *Liber de Ludo Aleae* by Gerolamo Cardano.

For more information on marked cards and how to detect them, consult *Gambling Scams* by Darwin Ortiz,

1984, and *Casino Game Protection* by Steve Forte, 2004.

For some fabulous, advanced trickery with marked cards, the definitive work to date is *Marked for Life* by Kirk Charles, 2002, Hermetic Press.

Card Concealer: I conceived of hiding objects *in* a deck of cards during a visit to the Spy Museum in Washington, D.C. In the gift shop there you can find many other household objects doctored to hide secret booty, but none (in my opinion) is as *unsuspecting as a pack of cards.*

# CHAPTER 5
# CHEAP TRICKS

Tearing a Deck in Half: This stunt goes back at least as far as 1909. See T. Nelson Downs, *The Art of Magic,* 1909, p. 24. John Northern Hilliard was the ghostwriter for this classic book.

Interestingly, it is possible to tear a deck in half without preparing the deck with a saw. The technique involves beveling the pack before you start, so that the initial tear goes through only a small quantity of cards. Another old method for deck tearing is to bake the deck in an oven for a limited amount of time (don't try this at home), which makes the cards more brittle and easier to tear.

Shiners: The use of shiners by gambling cheats dates back at least as far as 1530. They're also called "light."

Can Cards Tell Time?: The anomaly about sum of the letters in the names of the thirteen values equaling 52 described in the third bullet point is included here courtesy of Max Maven.

Back Breaker: Magician Pat Hazell invented this amusing gag. See "Down the Falls, Up the Back," by Stephen Minch, *New York Magic Symposium: Collection Five,* 1986, p. 134.

Memorizing a Deck: The key card was first published in 1593 in the aforementioned *Giochi di Carte Bellissimi,* by Horatio Galasso.

# CHAPTER 6
# WILD CARDS

Card Condo: If building card castles interest you, you owe it to yourself to check out the work of Bryan Berg in *Stacking the Deck* (with Thomas O'Donnell). This book chronicles Bryan Berg's amazing construction talents with a deck of cards: He builds skyscrapers, houses, and replicas of famous buildings, often utilizing more than 20,000 cards.

Fortune-Telling: European gypsies first adapted cards to the tarot. The oldest surviving pack of tarot cards dates from the 15th century and was created for the Duke of Milan. This dates the tarot to two centuries *after* the first playing cards. Surprisingly, tarot cards were not originally intended for foretelling the future. Like the playing cards they descended from, tarot cards were originally used for gaming.

# CHAPTER 7
# SAFE BETS

Flipped: The standard title for this classic stunt is "The Circus Card Trick." The originator is unknown, but in references starting around 1940, it is always described as being very old. For more, see Fred Braue and Jean Hugard, *The Royal Road to Card Magic,* 1949, p. 138.

Joker Is on You!: Though these are playing card variations of "Nim," a mathematical con that dates back to at least the 16th century. The game is normally played with matchsticks or stones. This card game can be played with other prime number quantities. (The version presented here uses 14, but the Joker is not in play, so the total in use is actually 13.) The most common is 31, as the effect is often referred to as "The Game of 31" or "The Australian Game of 31" (though there is no known evidence that it originated Down Under). The original source is not clear; there are indications it may go back several hundred years, and it is at least traceable to the 19th century, where it was probably most often used at racetracks.

Stepping Through a Card: The earliest published record of this classic stunt appears to be in Richard Neve's *The Merry Companion: or, Delights for the Ingenious* (1716). It is the first trick in the book (page 1) and called "To cut a Hole in a Playing-Card, big enough for a Man to creep through."

Three-Card Monte: Card expert Jason England offers the theory on the origins of the slang term "broad": Though some may claim the term refers to the Queen, it actually refers to the cards, in that the cards were literally "broader" than bridge (whist) cards of the day. Some old boxes actually say "broads" on the side. "Broads" became slang for all cards shortly thereafter. So "Broad-Tossers" are card tossers.

The earliest Monte citation dates back to 1408, in France.

The Bent Corner Ruse: The bent corner gambit was first published in 1872.

"What is the oldest surviving deck of cards?": See Leo Behnke, *The Making of Playing Cards,* Lybrary.com edition, 2005, p. 7.

"Are cards illegal?": See W. Benham Gurney, *Playing Cards: The History and Secrets of the Pack,* Spring Books, London, date unknown, p. 1.

See also: *Secrets of Playing Cards,* History Channel documentary, 2007.

## FOREWORD

David Blaine is a magician who has elevated the art of magic and is best known for living in very strange places (block of ice, water tank, small boxes).

## LAST WORDS

"Take Care and Take Cards." Thanks to magician Steve Beam for permission to use this phrase, with which he closed every issue of The Trapdoor during his 15-year tenure as editor.

# Index

## A

According to Hoyle, 162–163
ace(s), 58, 60, 66–67, 86, 115, 131, 152
    of diamonds, 17
    four, 50–53, 85, 162
    of hearts, 55
    of spades, 188
    stamp on, 27
Alamo, 173
Aleister Crowley tarot card deck, 144, 154
Alexander the Great, 92
antiquated grip. See missing finger deal
*Archivo General de Indias,* 163
*Art of Astonishment, Volume One*
    (Sankey), 99

## B

Back Breaker, 142–143
Barely Lift a Finger, 58–60
    on DVD, 58–60
    variation on, 60
"basement" dealing, practice for, 171
Bayer, David, 93
Beam, Steve, 39, 75
Bent Corner Ruse, The, 160, 184–185
    "broad tosser" in, 184
    "shills" in, 184
    wallman in, 184
Berg, Bryan, 157
Bernardino of Sienna, (saint), 182
"best bower," 89
betting games, 160–185
Bicycle Card Co., 188
Blaine, David, vii
blank backs
    edgework with, 18
    smudges on, 18
Blank Fan, on DVD, 17–18
blockout technique, 113, 116
Bowie, Jim, 173
Bradáč, Zdeněk, 97
Bridge, The, on DVD, 88–89
Britland, David, 125, 132, 161
Buck, Dan
    flourishes by, 189
    website of, 189
Buck, Dave
    flourishes by, 189
    website of, 189

## C

calendar, Aztec, 150
"canceled" casino deck, 38, 67, 97
Card Box Balance, 155
Card Calendar, 150–151
Card Calisthenics, variation on,
    158–159
Card Cascade, 6, 33–35, 142
card castles, 146–149
    tallest, 157
    world records for, 157
Card Concealer, 121–122
Card Condo, 146–149
card counting, device for, 161
"card cutting," 99, 112, 121–122, 123,
    124
card flourish, 7–37, 88–89
    effortless, 24
    one v. two-handed, 22
    purpose of, 34
    web site for, 189
card games, 1
    can't lose, 126–143
card on forehead, 159
Card Punch, 120
Card Quiz
    on Canada Bill, 185
    on card construction, 43
    on card illegality, 182
    on cards farthest thrown, 31
    on cards with maps, 149
    on cascade trick, 35
    on deck printing, 47
    on explosives, 57
    on eyes, 188
    on indexes, 16
    on largest card fan, 21
    on memorizing decks, 134
    on Nine of Diamonds, 14
    on nutritional value, 105
    on oldest deck, 163
    on playing card origination, 25
    on "playing without a full deck," 27
    on real kings, 92
    on Solitaire Encryption Algorithm,
        54
    on tallest card building, 157
    on telling time, 151
    on Texas emancipation, 173
    on unshuffling, 97
    on valuable decks, 53
Card Ruler, 156–157
Card Shark, The, on DVD, 40–43
Card Shaving, device for, 123
card shoe, 23. *See also* "Two Shoe" card
    shoe
card tricks, 3–4, 39–60, 125–143
    for the blind, 61
Cards in a Bottle, 104–105, 106
*carreau* (diamond), 25
"cartomancy," 152
casino shuffles, 71, 93
    riffle for, 75–77
Catch-a-Deck, 28–29
    variation of, 29
cavalier, 102
Charlemagne, King, 92
Charlier, 24
"Charming Cheat." *See* Nash, Martin A.
cheats, 18, 35, 43, 96, 99, 114, 128,
    132–133, 161
    card punch for, 120
    grips for, 171
    holdout devices for, 164–165
    jail for, 182
    K.C. Card Company for, 116
    marked cards for, 113–115
    with overhand shuffle, 82
    shaved cards for, 123
    three-card Monte for, 181–185
chest holdout device, 165
Christmas Card, 68–69
Cleveland State University, 31
Close, Michael, 100
*coeur* (heart), 25
con men, 168, 181
conversation piece, 104–105

"cooler," 165
Crockett, Davy, 173
crooked deal, 186
Crowley, Aleister, 144, 154
"Curse of Scotland," the, 14

# D

Dalrymple, John, Sir, 14
daub, 128
David, King, 92
Dead Man's Hand, 131
Dealer's Grip, 5
dealing from bottom. *See* "basement"
    dealing
deceptions, with callouts, 4
deck-switching device, 165
Devil's prayer book/picture book, The.
    *See* playing cards
Diaconis, Persi, 93
diazo dye, 57
difficulty rating, 2
*Discoverie of Witchcraft* (Scot), 7
*Don't Bet on It* (Garcia), 181
Double Bridge, The, on DVD, 90–91
Dovetail Shuffle, 88
DVD, 2
    Barely Lift a Finger, 58–60
    Blank Fan, 17–18
    Bridge, 88–89
    Card Shark, 40–43
    Double Bridge, 90–91
    Fake Marked Cards, 126–128
    False Cut, 96–97
    Faro Shuffle, 83–85
    Flipped, 168–171
    Friction Four, 66–67
    Getting Mental, 137–140
    Giant Fan, 19–21
    Hindu Shuffle, 72–74
    In-the-Hands Riffle Shuffle, 78–80
    Memorizing a Deck, 134–136
    No-Handed Flip, 11–12
    No-Handed Flip Plus, 13–14
    One Ahead, 44–47
    One-Handed Cut, 24–25
    One-Handed Fan, 22–23
    One-Handed Flip, 10
    Overhand Shuffle, 81–82
    Pointer Power, 55–57
    Presto Prediction, 62–64
    Ribbon Spread and Flip, 8–9
    Tabled Riffle Shuffle, 75–77
    Self-Cutting Deck, 26–27
    Throwing Cards, 30–31

# E

Effective Playing Cards, 95
eight, 131, 153
Electric Deck, 35
*euchre* card, 89
*euchre* game, 89

# F

Fake Marked Cards, on DVD, 126–128
False Cut, 40, 50, 96–97
    on DVD, 96–97
Faro Shuffle, 19, 83–85, 88, 90, 189. *See
    also* One-Handed Faro Shuffle
    on DVD, 83–85
    magicians using, 85
    out-, 85
    perfect, 85
    stacking four aces with in-, 85
    variation of, 85
Finding Four Aces Without Touching
    the Deck, 50–53
variation on, 53
finger placement, 5
five, 153
    of clubs, 55
    of hearts, 55
Flicked, 180
Flipped, on DVD, 168–171
force, card
    hindu shuffle for, 74
    ten-twenty, 48–49, 53, 112
Fortune-Telling, card meanings in,
    152–154
four, 152
French, 102
    suits by, 25
Friction Four, on DVD, 66–67

# G

*Gambling Scams* (Ortiz), 184
Garcia, Frank, monte pitch of, 181
Gazzo, 125, 132, 161
geographical cards, 149
Georgia State University, 150

Getting Mental, on DVD, 137–140
Giant Fan, 19–21, 85
    on DVD, 19–21
    largest, 21
    variation on, 21
"glims." *See* Shiners
glycerin, 57
Grant, U.F., 128
Groves, Tom, 134
Guinness World Records, 157

# H

hands, importance of, 4
Hardy, Richard, 27
Hart, Samuel, 89
Haydn, Whit, 61
Henry VIII, 92
Hernández, José, 113
Hindu Shuffle, 72–74
    with card force, 74
    on DVD, 72–74
Hofzinser, Johann, 65
Hofzinser card, 65
holdout devices, 164–165
    chest, 165
    deck switching, 165
    Keplinger, 164
    Martin, 164
Houston, Sam, 173
Hu, David, 12

# I

indices, card, 5, 16, 17, 102–103
instructive cards, 149
International Brotherhood of
    Magicians, The, website of, 189
International Playing Card Society,
    website of, 189
In-the-Hands Riffle Shuffle, 75, 78–80,
    88
    on DVD, 78–80
Isle of Man, 149

# J

Jack of the Trump Suit. *See* "best
    bower"
jacks, 102–103, 115, 153
    one-eyed, 188
Jay, Joshua, 39, 187, 189

Jay, Ricky, 31, 86
Joker Is on You, troubleshooting for, 172–173
jokers, 89, 188. *See also jucker* (joker)
Jones, Canada Bill, 161
  as "tosser," 185
*jucker* (joker), 89
Judith, 92
Julius Caesar, 92

# K

K.C. Card Company
  for cheats, 116
  marked decks from, 116
"Keplinger" holdout, 164
"key" card, 134–136, 168
king, 102, 115, 153
  of clubs, 92
  of diamonds, 92, 188
  of hearts, 92, 188
  of spades, 92
  knave, 102

# L

Laue, Ralf, 21
*Le Musée Français de la Carte à Jouer*, website of, 189
Leap Frog, The, 98, 100–103
learning, in order, 2
Leclerc, Eric, 106
left handers, 5, 17
linoid finish, 141
luminous readers, 114

# M

magic, 34
  societies for, 189
*Magic: The Complete Course* (Jay), 189
*MAGIC* magazine, 39
magic tricks, 1, 34
marked cards for, 113–115
magicians, 7, 30, 32, 39, 61, 65, 77, 93, 96, 100, 158, 168, 189
  card force by, 48–49, 74
  card handling by, 34–35
  faro shuffle for, 85
  multiple outs by, 62–64
  one-ahead principle by, 44–47
  shuffle, 71

Mamet, David, 187
Mamluk people, card suits of, 25
Marked Miracle, 117–119
Marking Cards, 18, 113–115. *See also* Fake Marked Cards
  blockout technique of, 113, 116
  device for, 116
  "scratching" for, 113–114
  subtlety for, 114
  tactilely, 120
  variations of, 115
"marks," 168
*Martin Fierro* (Hernández), 113
"Martin" holdout, 164
Massacre of Glencoe, 14
materials list, 2
Maugham, Somerset, 39
McCall, Jack, 131
Memorizing a Deck, 134–136
  on DVD, 134–136
  world record of, 134
Metropolitan Museum of Art, The, 53
Middleton, Richard, 50
misdirection, 4
missing finger deal, 171
*Mr. Know All* (Maugham), 39
multiple outs, 62–64
Murphy, Weasel, 171

# N

Nash, Martin A., 77
nine, 153. *See also* "Curse of Scotland," the
  of diamonds, 14
  of spades, 55
No-Handed Flip, on DVD, 11–12
No-Handed Flip Plus, on DVD, 13–14
Northbrooke, John, 182

# O

O'Brien, Dominic, 134
One Ahead, on DVD, 44–47
one-ahead principle, 44–47
One-Handed Cut, on DVD, 24–25
One-Handed Fan, 21, 22–23, 78
  on DVD, 22–23
  variation, 23
One-Handed Faro Shuffle, 86–87
One-Handed Flip, on DVD, 10
origami, 100

Ortiz, Darwin, 184
Osbourne, Ozzy, 173
Ose, Jay, 96
"outjogging," 19
Overhand Shuffle, 56, 75, 81–82
  cheating with, 82
  on DVD, 81–82
  randomization with, 93

# P

"Paris" kings, 92
pasteboards, parts of, 5
*Phantoms of the Card Table* (Britland, Gazzo), 125, 132
pip, 5
*pique* (spade), 25
Playing Card Company, U.S., 29, 80
Playing Card Purse, 110
Playing Card Wallet, 107–110
variation on, 110
playing cards. *See also* pasteboards, parts of
  assumptions for, 4
  braille, 61
  chemical coating on, 105, 141
  condition of, 2, 15
  construction of, 43, 65
  cuts for, 24–27
  encryption method with, 54
  English tax stamp on, 27
  European, 5, 102
  fans, 15–23
  form/terminology of, 5
  geographical, 149
  handcrafted, 112
  on hat, 173
  history of, 189
  illegality of, 182
  index on, 5, 16, 17, 102–103
  instructive, 149
  marked, 18, 113–115, 116, 120
  origination of, 25
  pointer, 55–57
  ribbon spreads/flips for, 8–14
  rich, 115
  skin adherence to, 159
  small maps on, 80
  "soft" corners of, 185
  tarot cards and, 144, 152, 154, 159
  telling time, 151
  as tools of deception, 125

unsolved crimes on, 95
U.S., 5, 47
valuable, 53
*Playing Cards* (Mamet), 187
*Playing Cards* (Sultan), 86
pointer cards, 55–57
Pointer Power, on DVD, 55–57
Post Card, 111–112
   variations on, 112
potassium permanganate, 57
practice, 2, 33–35, 36–37, 83
   "basement" dealing, 171
   Ultimate Catch, 36–37
Presto Prediction, on DVD, 62–64
*Professional Gambler's Handbook*, The
   (Murphy), 171

## Q

queen, 102, 115, 153, 160, 181–185
   of hearts, 92

## R

"readers." *See* Marking Cards
Really Shuffle the Cards, 93–95
Ribbon Spread and Flip, The, 8–9, 94
on DVD, 8–9
"rich" cards, 115
Robbins, Tom, 57
Rowland, Ian, 112
royal flush, 40, 43, 162

## S

San Jacinto battle, 173
Sankey, Jay, 99
Satan, 181
Scaife, Lawrence, 114
scaling. *See* Throwing Cards
Scarne, John, 23
Schneier, Bruce, 54
Scot, Reginald, 7
Self-Cutting Deck, on DVD, 26–27
*Semi-Automatic Card Tricks, Volume 2*
   (Beam), 39, 75
seven, 153
   of diamonds, 55
sharks, card, 43, 50
sharper, card, 43, 161
shills, 184
Shiners, 132–133

cell phone as, 132
shuffling, 71–97. *See also* Buck,
   Dan; Buck, Dave
bridge, 88–89
casino, 71, 75–77, 93
double bridge, 90–91
dovetail, 88
false, 71
faro, 19, 83–85, 88, 90, 189
gentle, 77
hindu, 72–74
in-the-hands, 75, 78–80, 88
magician, 71
one-handed faro, 86–87
overhand, 56, 75, 81–82, 93
perfect, 86
really, 93–95
riffle, 70, 75–77, 81, 88, 93
seven times, 93
six, 153
sleight of hand, 4, 31, 71, 113, 158, 168
   blind, 29
   smoothness for, 34
Smith, Rick, 31
snake locomotion, 12
Society of American Magicians, The,
   website of, 189
solitaire, 54
Solitaire Encryption Algorithm, 54
Sotheby's, London, 53
South Carolina Department of
   Corrections, The, 95
*Spotlight on the Card Sharp* (Scaife),
   114
Springer, Jerry, 184
Stacking Four Aces, in-faro shuffles
   for, 85
stacking the deck, 96
Stanford University, 93
static electricity, 141
Static Sting, 141
Stepping Through a Card, 176–179
*Still Life with Woodpecker* (Robbins), 57
Sultan, Donald, 86
Swain, James, 1

## T

Tabled Riffle Shuffle, 70, 75–77, 81, 88
   on DVD, 75–77
   randomization with, 93
tarot cards, 152, 159

of Aleister Crowley, 144, 154
tarot reader, 152
Tearing a Deck in Half, 129–130
ten, 115, 153
"Ten Greatest Card Tricks of All Time,
   The," 189
Ten-Twenty Force, The, 48–49, 53,
   74, 112
three, 152
   of spades, 55
Three Fingers Willie, 128
Three-Card Monte, 181–183. *See also*
   Bent Corner Ruse, The; "tosser"
Three's a Crowd, 166–167
Throwing Cards, 30–31
   on DVD, 30–31
   expert on, 32
   farthest, 31
Throwing Cards Into a Hat, 174–175
Thurston, Howard, 30, 32
"toss," the, 183, 185. *See also* Bent
   Corner Ruse, The; Three-Card
   Monte; "tosser"
"tosser," 181–183
   broad, 184
*trèfle* (club), 25
"Triplicates," 16
Turner, Richard, 29
*21st Century Card Magic* (Swain), 1
"twinkles." See Shiners
two, 152
"Two Shoe" card shoe, viii, 23
Two-Handed Fan, 15–16, 17, 19, 21

## U

Ultimate Catch, The, practice for, 36–37
Union Pacific Railroad, 185
United States Capitol Building, 157
United States Postal Service, 111
unshuffling/sorting, world record for, 97

## W

wallman, 184
Warm Springs Correctional Center, 97
Waterfall. *See* Card Cascade
Wild Bill Hickok, 131
wild cards, 145
World Series of Poker, 187
Worthy, Morgan, 150
wow cards, 112
Wright, Steven, 145

ℰ ℭ

Behold, four Kings in majesty rever'd,
With hoary whiskers and a forky beard;
And four fair Queens whose hands sustain a flow'r,
Four Knaves in garbs succinct, a trust band,
Caps on their heads, and halberds in their hand;
And particolour'd troops, a shining train,
Draw forth to combat on the velvet plain.

With his broad sabre next, a chief in years,
The hoary Majesty of Spades appears,
Puts forth one manly leg, to sight reveal'd,
The rest, his many-colour'd robe conceal'd.
The rebel Knave, who dares his prince engage,
Proves the just victim of his royal rage.
Ev'n mighty Pam [*Knave of Clubs*], that Kings and Queens o'erthrew
And mow'd down armies in the fights of Lu,
Sad chance of war! now destitute of aid,
Falls undistinguish'd by the victor spade!

—ALEXANDER POPE, *The Rape of the Lock,* 1712